THE SEASONS *of* NEW ENGLAND

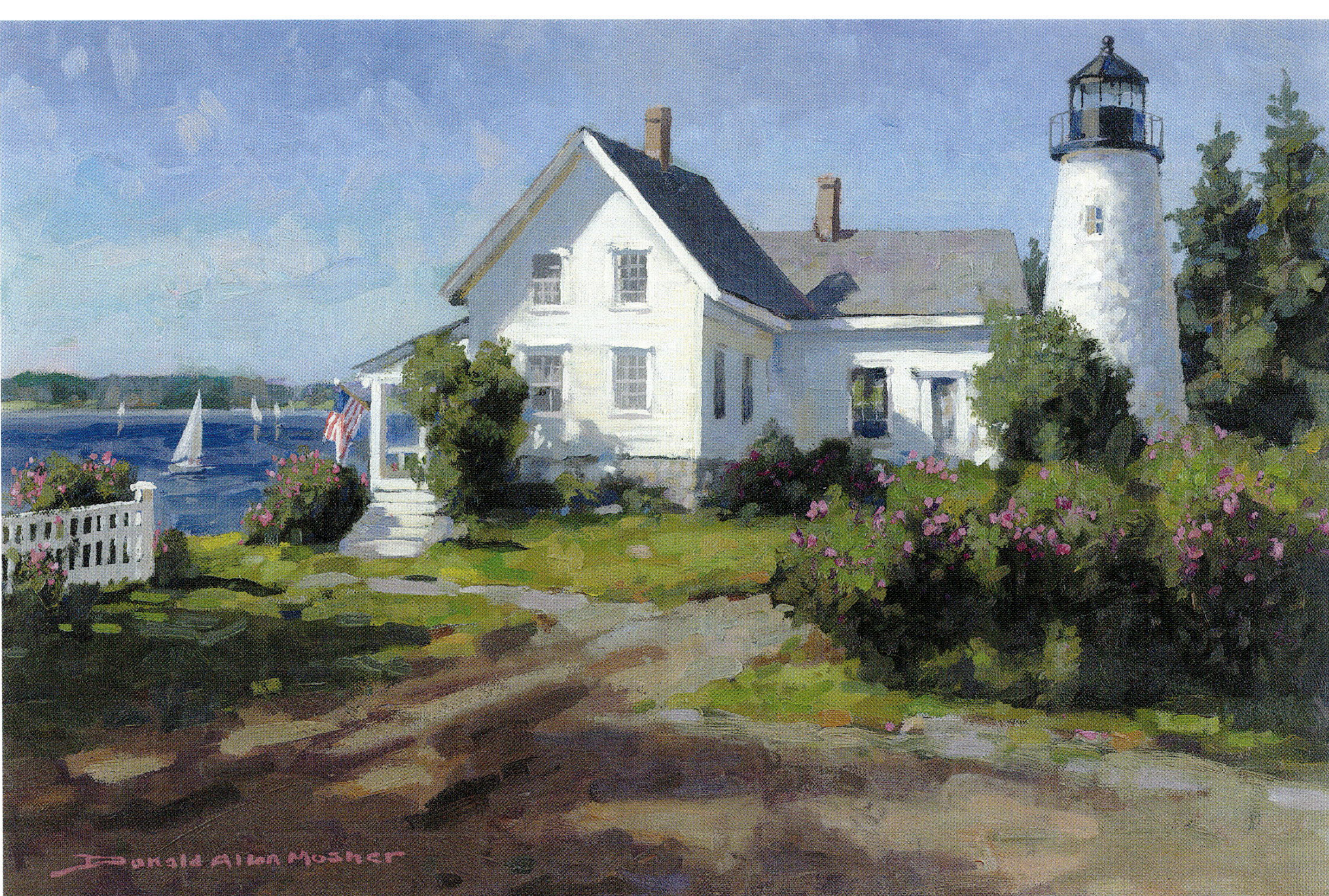
Donald Allan Mosher

THE SEASONS *of* NEW ENGLAND

LANDSCAPE PAINTINGS OF DONALD ALLEN MOSHER

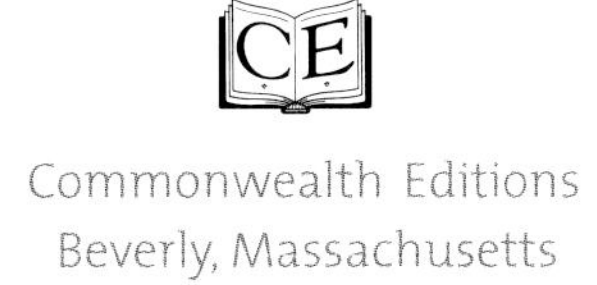

Commonwealth Editions
Beverly, Massachusetts

Cover & interior design by Judith Arisman.

Printed in Hong Kong.
Published by Commonwealth Editions, an imprint of Memoirs Unlimited, Inc., 266 Cabot Street, Beverly, MA 01915.

Visit our Web site:
www.commonwealtheditions.com

Cover: Winter, Pigeon Cove, Rockport (25 x 30)
Frontispiece: Dice Head Light, Castine, Maine (16 x 22)

Many of the images in this book are available as fine art prints or as glicée prints at the Mosher Gallery.

Contents

I dedicate this book to Christine—my muse, my wife, and the greatest friend I will ever have in this world.

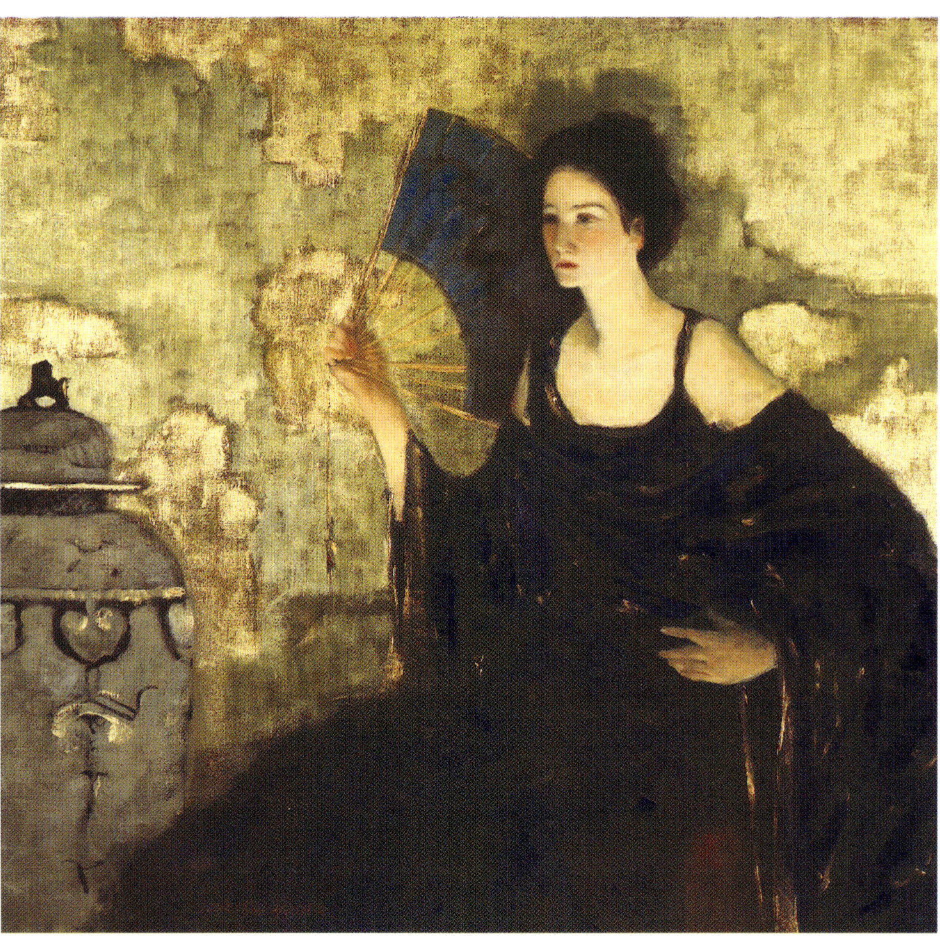

Lady in Blue by Christine Mosher
(24 x 24)

Foreword

The fabric of existence weaves itself whole. You cannot set art off in the corner and hope for it to have vitality, reality, and substance. . . . It comes directly out of the heart of experience of life and thinking about life and living life.
—Charles Ives

More than twenty years ago, a young artist came into my Rockport gallery. We found we had a lot in common. We both had started out professionally as watercolorists, and we often discussed our favorite watercolor painters—Sargent, Homer, and Hopper, as well as English watercolor masters. They were constantly in our conversations.

In 1981, Don Mosher and his wife, Christine, opened their gallery on Main Street in Rockport. Shortly thereafter, my wife, Gloria, and I began to see Don and Christine socially. This led to many trips, sometimes to museums and art exhibits. More often, we took painting trips throughout New England, plus several trips to the West Coast and Puerto Rico. This friendship expanded to taking trips abroad. We visited Italy, Greece, Austria, Hungary, the Czech Republic, Malta, and Tunisia.

Don has always impressed me with his ability to devote himself totally to the direction he has chosen as an artist. He has always been interested in maritime subjects; however, he not only expanded his subject matter but has also become a prominent oil painter, mastering the medium in remarkably few years.

Cape Ann has been a mecca for some of America's greatest artists, some taking up residence on the Cape, others visiting in the summer from New York, Boston, and as far away as the West Coast. The tradition of Cape Ann art endures. Don Mosher's contribution to this grand tradition is assured as this volume so aptly demonstrates.

—Tom Nicholas, N.A.
Rockport, Massachusetts

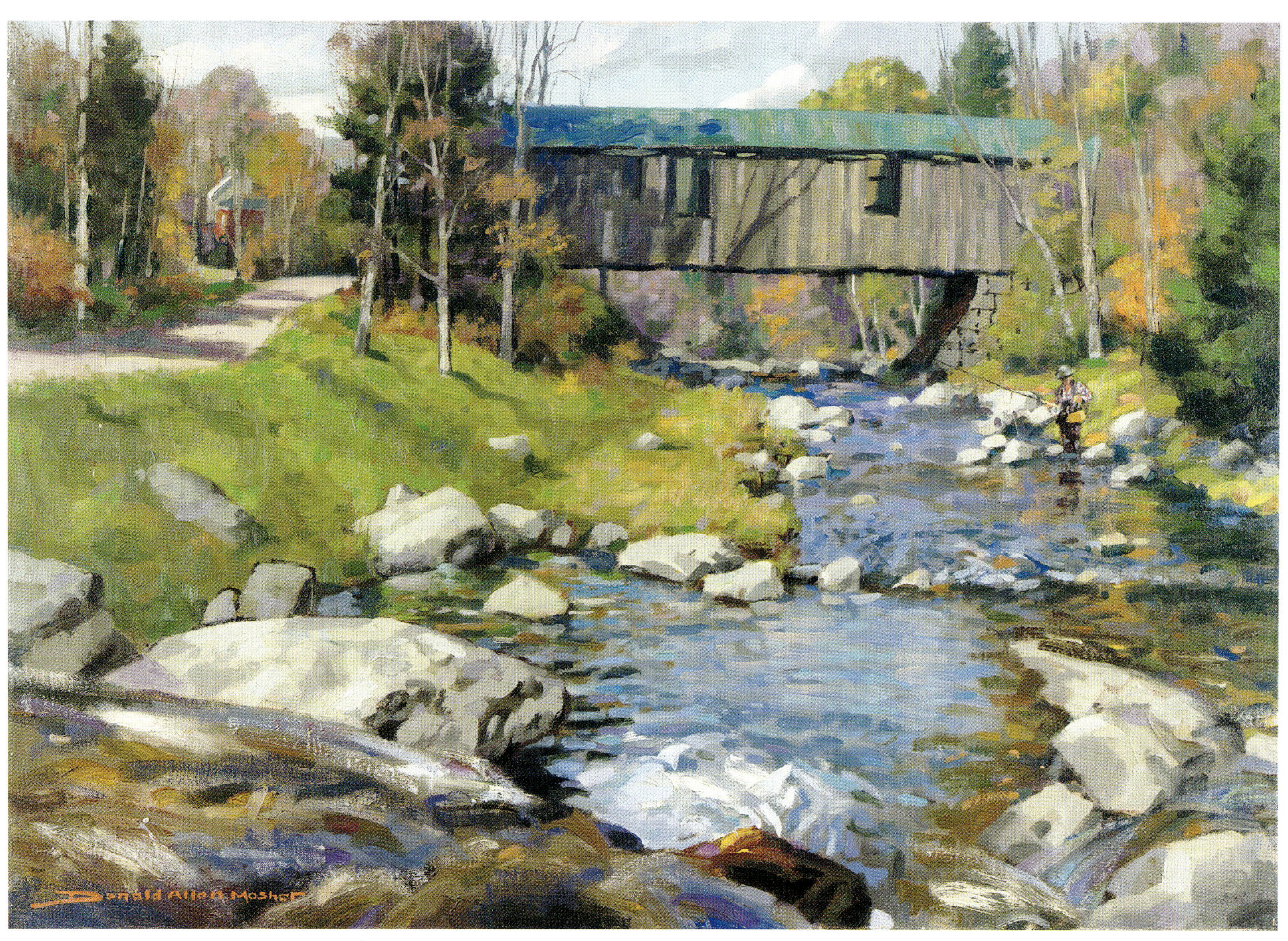

Fly Fishing in Jeffersonville, Vermont
(26 x 36)

INTRODUCTION

Get rhythm through a picture. See it as it comes together. Don't paint by part. Interrelate things. Art is in the joints—how shapes come together.

— Charles Movalli

As a boy, I was always drawing and doodling. When I was eight we moved to a new house in Topsfield with a full basement, where I drew Mickey Mouse cartoons all over the walls using charcoal briquettes. Mother was not too happy about this. I won my first art award when I was ten, drawing a dog for Be Kind to Animals Week.

Not much of an algebra or French student, I spent more time at the pool hall or on the football field than I did on homework. But our art teacher, "Mrs. Mac," encouraged me, and years later friends told me that I was the only one in our high school class who had known what he was going to do. I don't remember it that way. I don't think I had a clue what I really wanted. The line under my senior class picture in our yearbook reads, "Good luck to Don in his career in art or in the navy."

I never joined the navy, and I didn't have the money or grades to go to college, so I spent a year selling tools at Sears. I finally decided to take two nights a week at the Vesper George School of Art in Boston, which was all I could afford. A commercial art school that trained students mostly for careers in advertising, Vesper George also taught interior decorating, fashion design, and fine art. I thought I wanted to be a mechanical illustrator—drawing for medical journals and the like. After a year in night school I realized you can't learn anything about art working two nights a week, so the following year I went full time. I worked summer jobs, and drove a taxi nights and weekends, to pay for school and living expenses.

I met my wife-to-be, Christine Crivello, my senior year. I graduated in 1968, she in 1970. We were married in 1969, and our daughter, Heather, was born in 1971. My father-in-law, Salvatore Crivello, was probably the greatest early influence on me as a painter. A commercial artist and sign designer for Salem Sign Company, he was a serious fine artist who had studied with Emile Gruppe. Until he took me to Gloucester and exposed me to Cape Ann artists, the only thing I knew about Gloucester was that we played them in football. Salvatore took me to Emile Gruppe's demonstrations and opened my eyes to the world of Cape Ann.

To support our family, I took a job in the art department at Stop & Shop in South Boston, and after four years, I became art director at Rich's Department

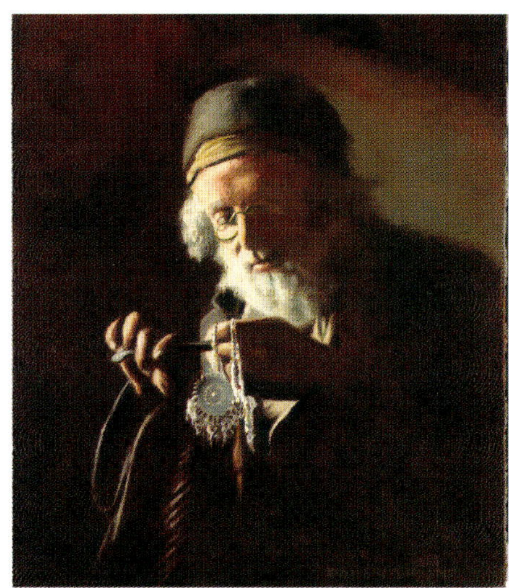

The Jewelry Crafstman (30 x 24), painted shortly after graduating from art school

Stores in Salem. All this time I taught painting in adult education classes at night and in our basement on Saturday mornings. We went out one night a week in those days. It was all we could afford.

In 1974 we opened a summer gallery on West Wharf in Rocky Neck. In 1981, we sold everything we had and mortgaged ourselves to the hilt to buy a Rockport restaurant no one wanted and convert it to a gallery. Interest rates were double-digit, but we bought the restaurant before we had even sold our previous home. It's the kind of thing you do when you're an artist.

Today, we have a home overlooking Rockport Harbor. My studio has high ceilings, a skylight, and a gas stove to keep me warm in four seasons, my 15 x 26 studio looks out on a perfect painting subject. I spend most of my time here—when I'm not painting on location or playing golf.

Rockport is like Topsfield was in the 1950s—or like many other New England communities of fifty or even one hundred years ago. Rockport is a throwback. There's no crime to speak of, no liquor for sale. Rockport is safe. Even at night, you can walk the streets alone without a thought. My wife calls it Mayberry. It is certainly worlds away from the art capital of the world, New York City, where our daughter is a successful interior designer.

Cape Ann is a throwback, and so am I. I like the old New England ways of sailing, fishing, farming, maple-sugaring—the way they did it in the old days with buckets and horse-drawn wagons, not the way it's done today with the intravenous drip method—plastic tubes connecting the trees. This is one of the reasons that artists for over a century have been attracted to Cape Ann and continue to come here today. When you visit Cape Ann, as thousands do on vacation each year, you find a life that's different from where you've come from. It's like stepping back in time.

Most of my paintings represent scenes that could have been painted fifty or even one hundred years ago. *Winter, Pigeon Cove, Rockport* is an example. There's nothing in it you wouldn't have seen in the 1950s—the same lobster boats, the same shacks, the same granite seawall. Maine also has a virtually unchanged seacoast, as does Martha's Vineyard's Menemsha Harbor.

This approach to painting may seem antiquated. We latter-day impressionists

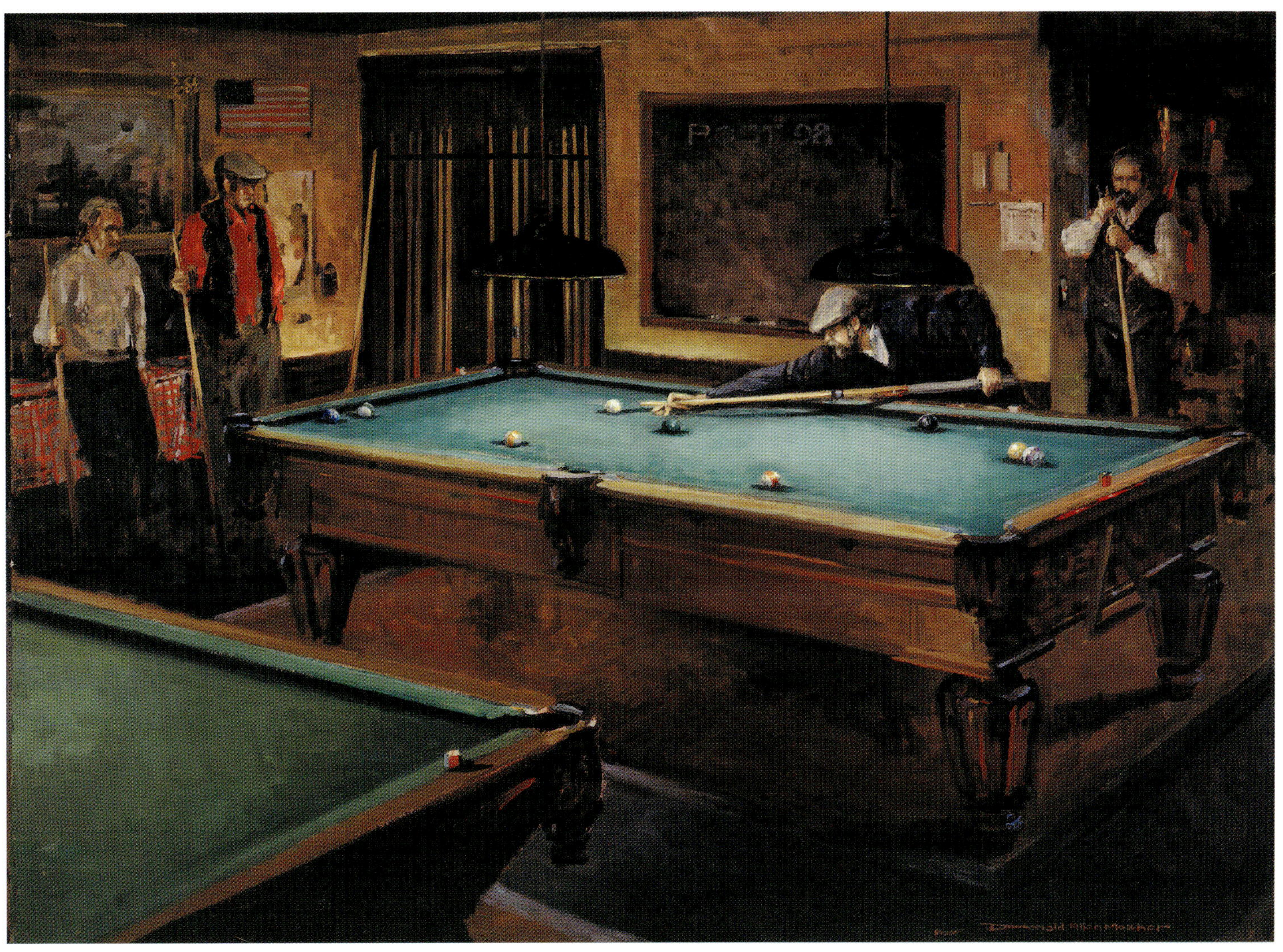

The Players: Continuation of a Misspent Youth (36 x 48)

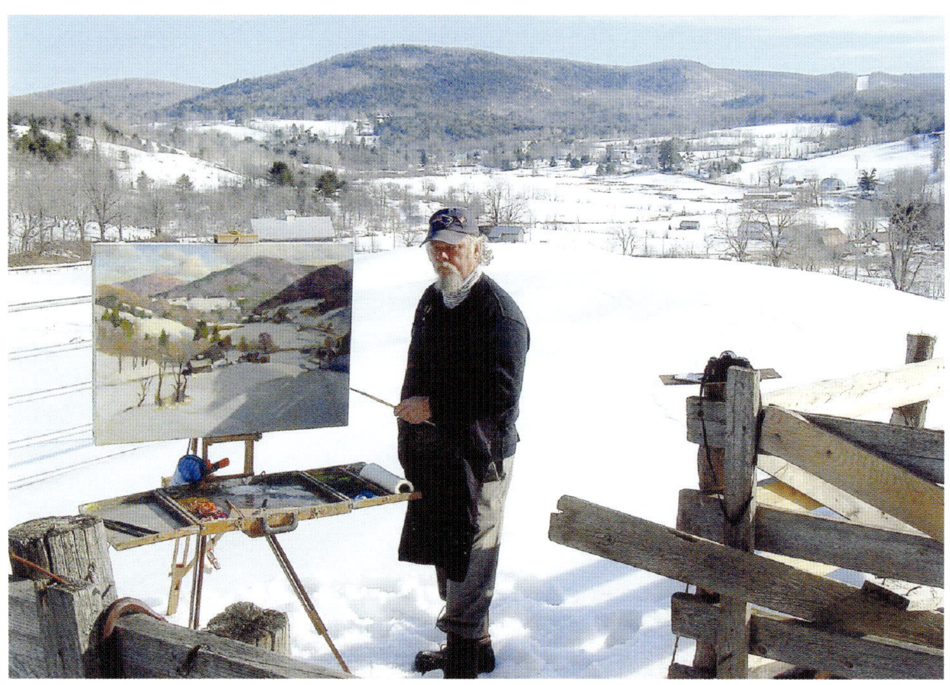

On location, Strafford, Vermont

may be painting subjects from a century ago, but then, so are today's moderns. Modern art, which started about 1910, isn't really modern anymore.

As the late Rockport artist Paul Strisik once told me, "There's nothing wrong with painting a subject that other artists paint. The thing is to paint it differently."

I appreciate the way the earliest painters painted. I think it's important to learn a modeled style of art. After all, even Picasso started out that way. I especially like the early Cape Ann painters, whose work is enjoying a renaissance today. Aldro Hibbard, Frederick Mulhaupt, William Lester Stevens, and others were a new generation of American impressionists. Hibbard was the best snow painter of them all, and I am flattered when my work is compared with his. Mulhaupt featured the wharves and schooners. I have tried to learn from these Cape Ann masters while putting my own stamp on the work.

Drawing closer to Cape Ann and its spirit, I also have been influenced by my contemporaries, like Don Stone, Paul Strisik, Charles Movalli, and Tom Nicholas. Nicholas has influenced me

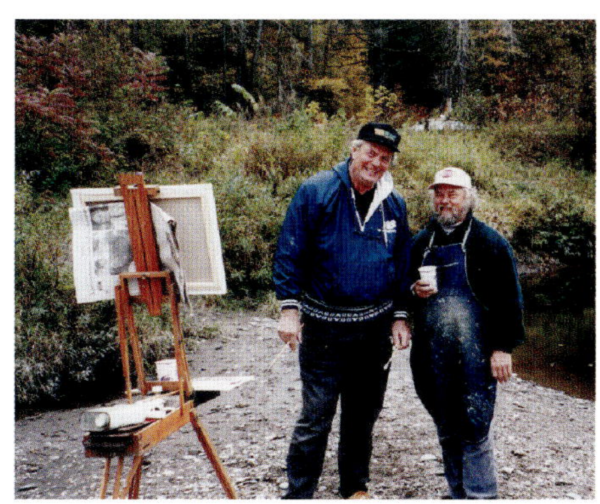

Taking a break from painting in Vermont with friend and fellow artist Tom Heinsohn (he's the tall one)

The viewer must learn to look at a picture as a graphic representation of a mood and not as a representation of objects.
—Wassily Kandinsky

perhaps more than any other, not in style so much as in artistic lifestyle. Through him and others who have generously shared their insights, I saw and began to understand the way an artist lives. I realized that the focus is always on the work. It is a disciplined life, wrapped up in art. When Christine and I are on vacation, we spend most of our time in museums and galleries.

A life in art is a strange journey. There are many people with talent, some with far more talent than I have. I was probably in the middle of the pack in art school. But something more than talent separates the artist from the pack. If there were eighty people in my class, I would say that at least sixty are no longer involved in art. Another fifteen, perhaps, are in commercial art. Only a handful are what are known as fine artists.

Being an artist is something that you have to do, or you can't do it. Art isn't just about talent. It's about desire, appreciation, and hard work. It's saying to yourself, I have to paint this painting. It's doing it because it has to be done.

Standing in the snow when the wind chill is below zero and painting for most of the day is hard work. But when you go somewhere warm at the end of the day, and you look at what you've accomplished, it's a feeling like none other in the world.

I would like to thank the following artists without whom my life would be drastically different. They are friends with whom I have painted on location. We enjoyed camaraderie, traded jokes, and shared stories of earlier artists. Each has been an inspiration to me, helping me to see the world as a better place: Tom Nicholas, John Terelak, Bill Fein, Charles Movalli, Dale Ratcliff, Don Stone, Paul Strisik, Ward Mann, Charles Umanita, T. M. Nicholas, Stapleton Kearns, John Nesta, Bernard Corey, Sal Grasso, Ivan Kamalic, Rudy Colao, Ken Knowles, Salvatore Crivello, and Michael Karas.

—Don Mosher
April 2003

THE SEASONS *of* NEW ENGLAND

Watercolors

Where the spirit does not work with the hand, there is no art.

—Leonardo da Vinci

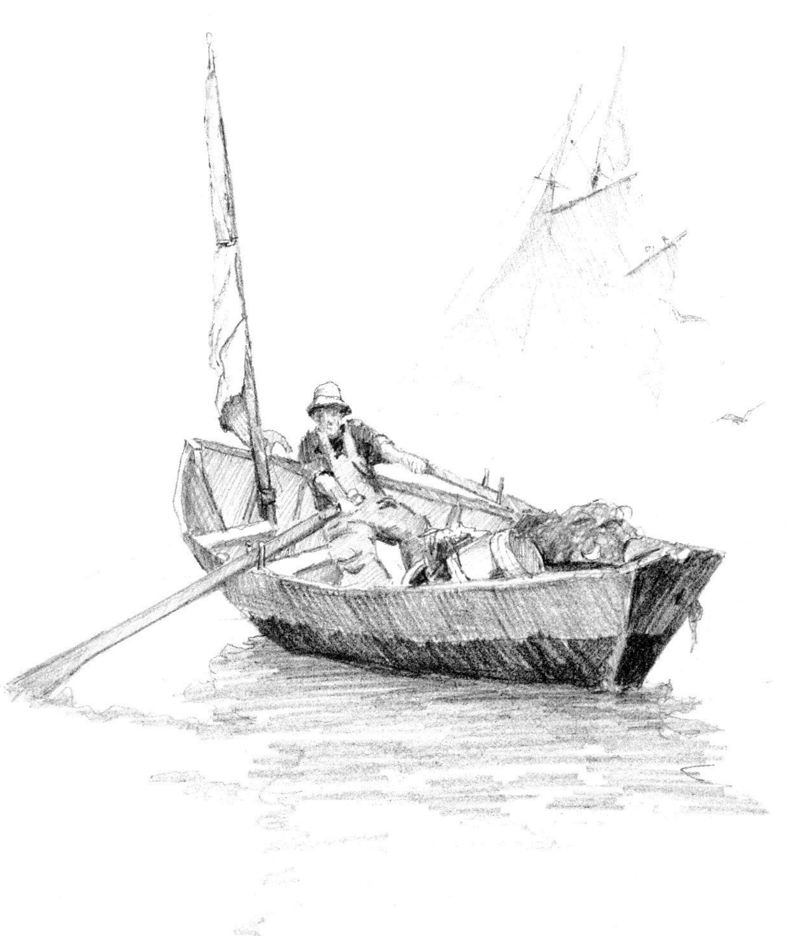

Early in my career, I learned that the artists who made a living from their work had an identifiable style—one you could spot a mile away. My wife encouraged me to focus on watercolors, and for eighteen years I painted almost exclusively in this medium.

Part of the excitement of working in watercolors is its uncertainty. Many times you will have what is called a happy accident, and occasionally it can be fun to take a painting in a surprising direction, but it is easier to make a mistake and ruin a painting with one false brush stroke. I don't like to use opaque white in my colors, so watercolors require much forethought and accurate drawing before painting begins.

I love the bright colors and freedom that oil paint provides, and the ability to make drastic changes in mid-painting. Still, there is nothing like a pure watercolor from the hand of a craftsman.

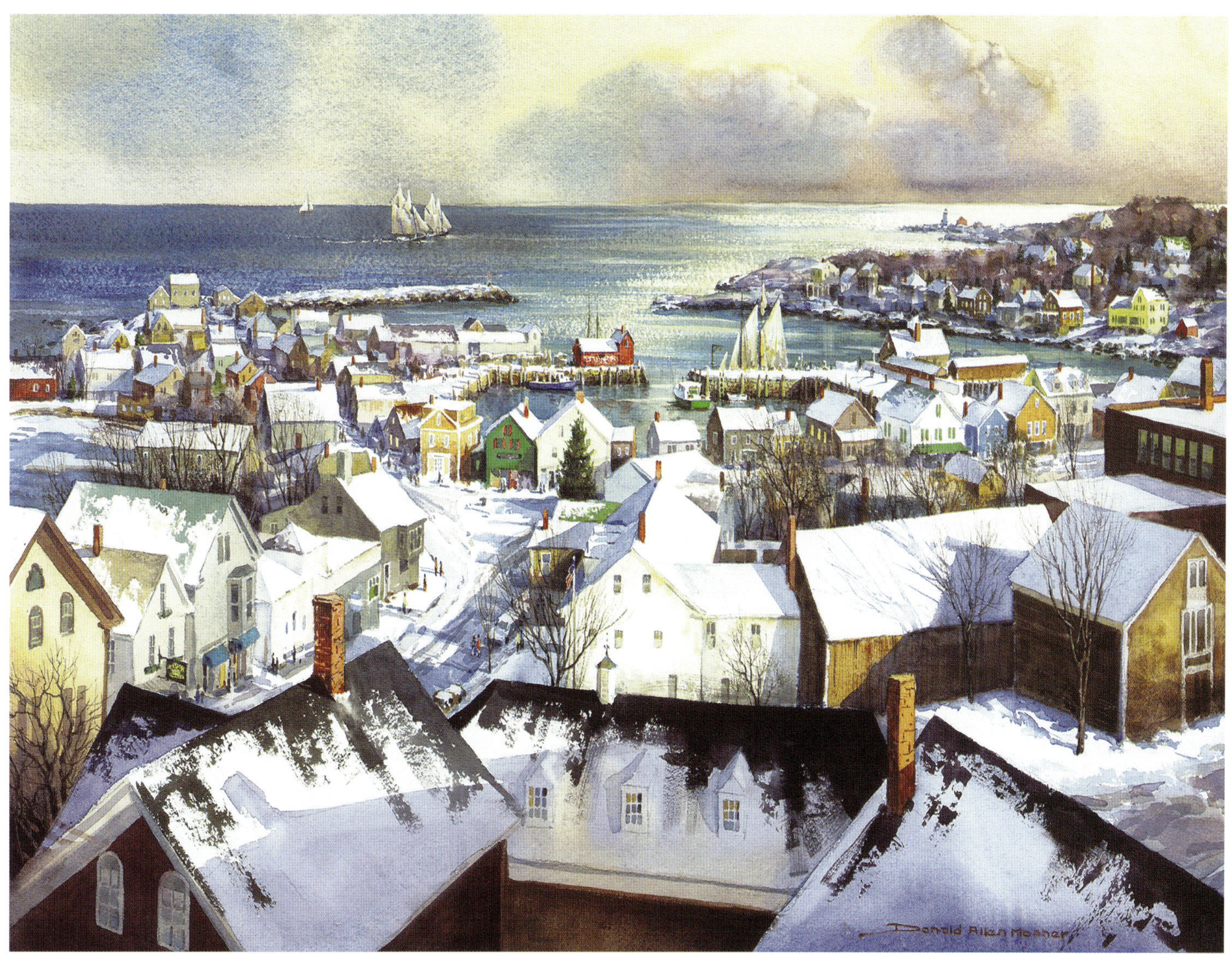

Rockport from the Old Sloop (20 x 30)

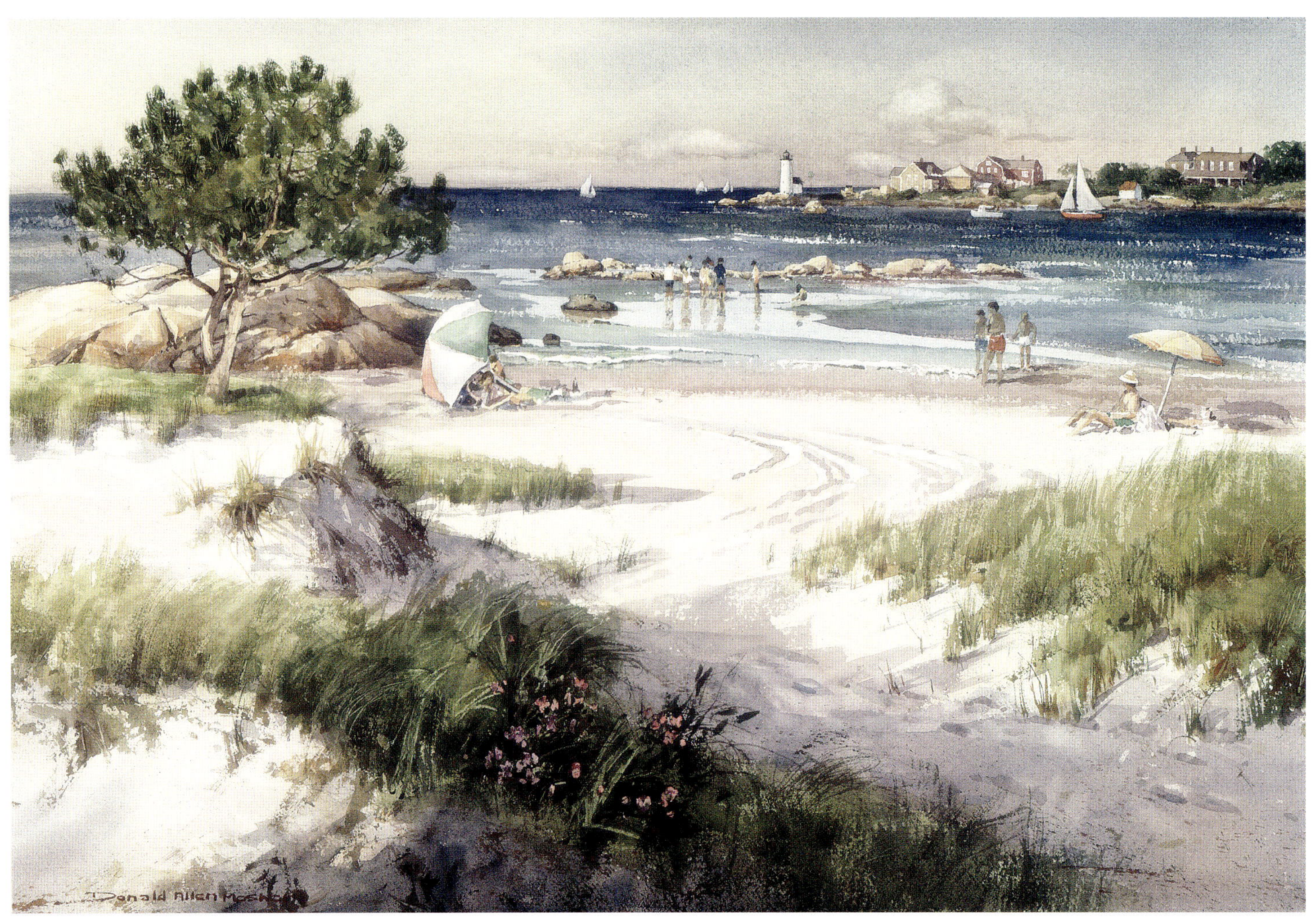

Cape Ann Summer (20 x 30)

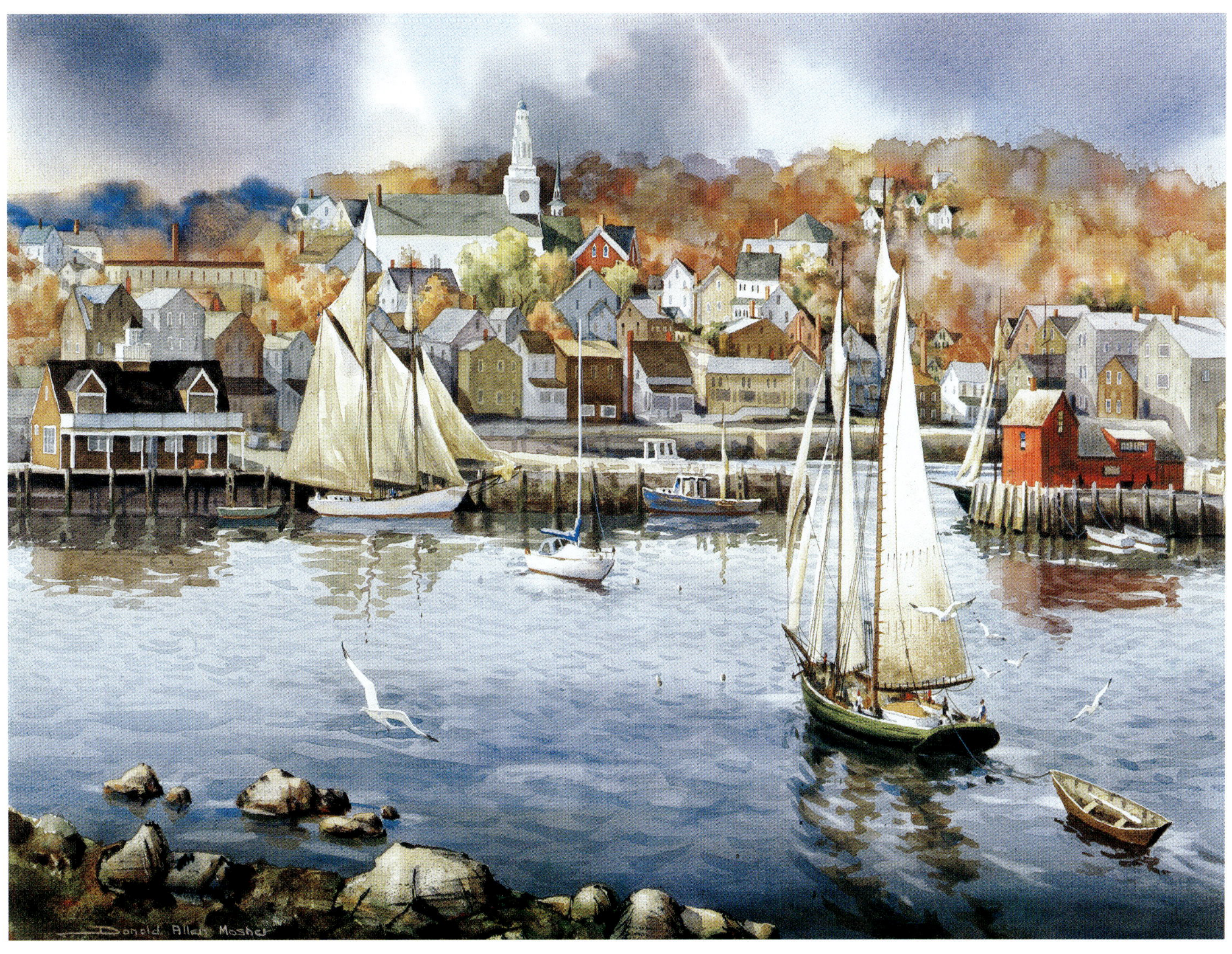

Rockport from the Headlands (22 x 30)

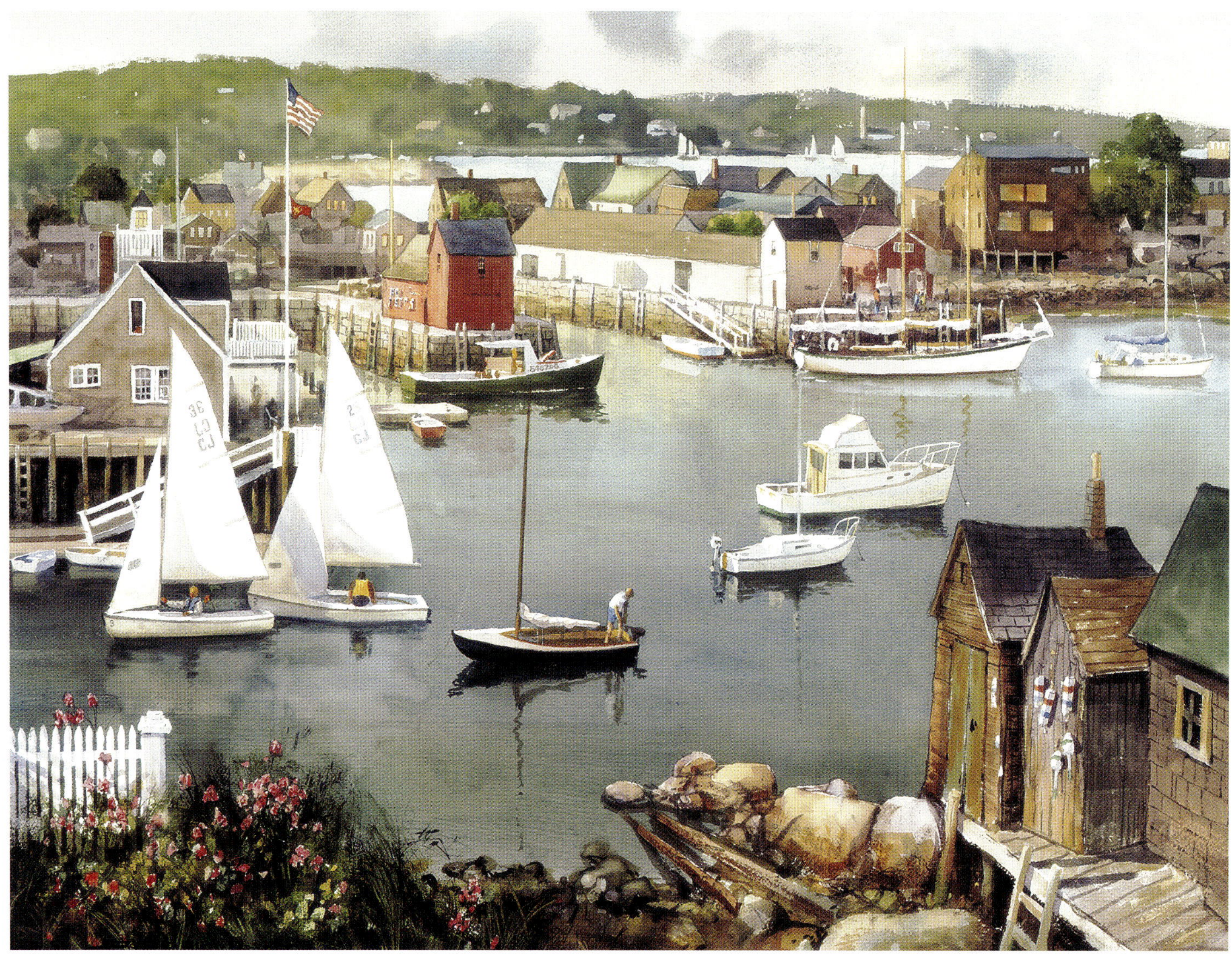

Spring Comes to Rockport (20 x 30)

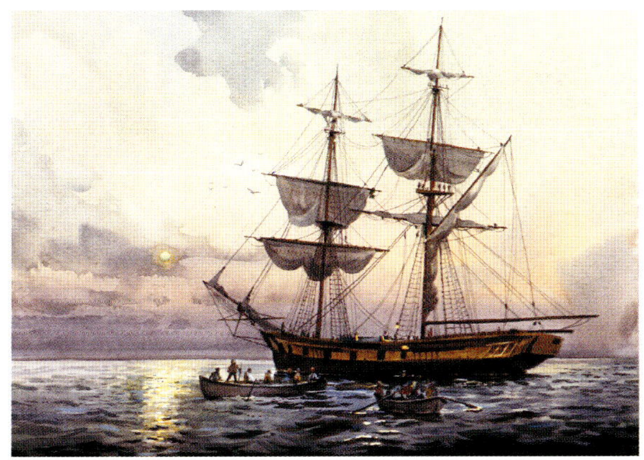

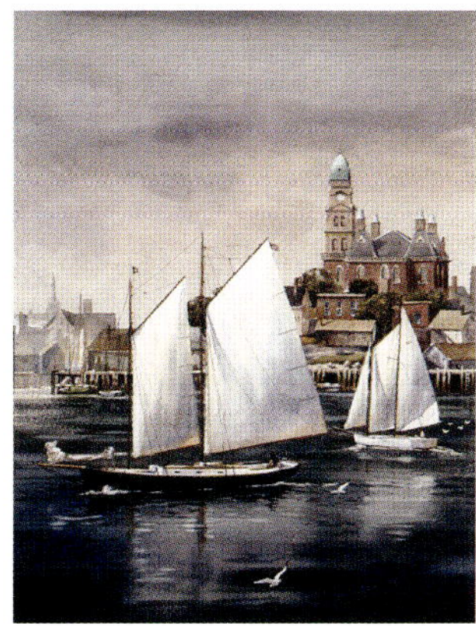

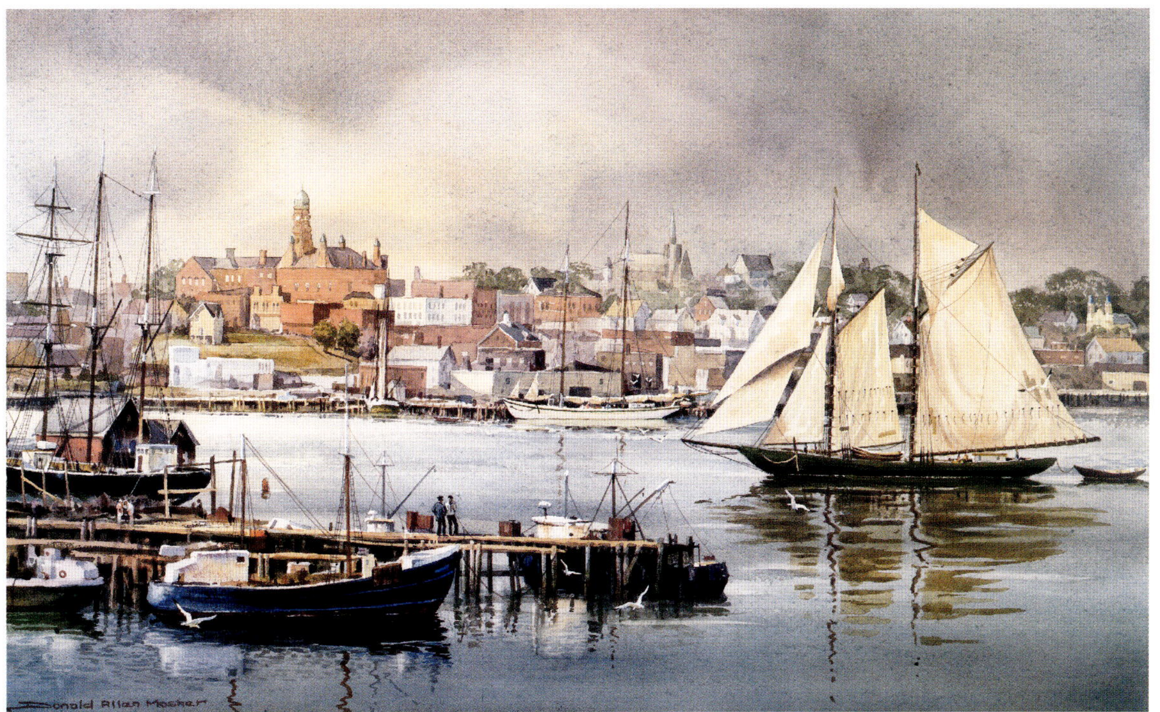

Top left: Sunset at Sea (12 x 15)
Top right: Harbor Cruise (16 x 11)
Bottom: Gloucester Harbor (18 x 30)

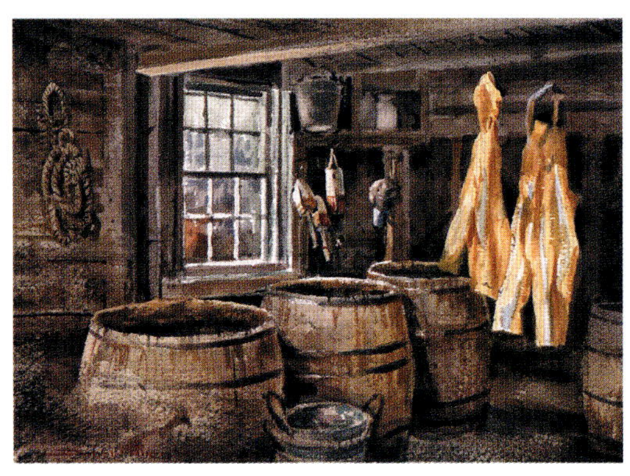

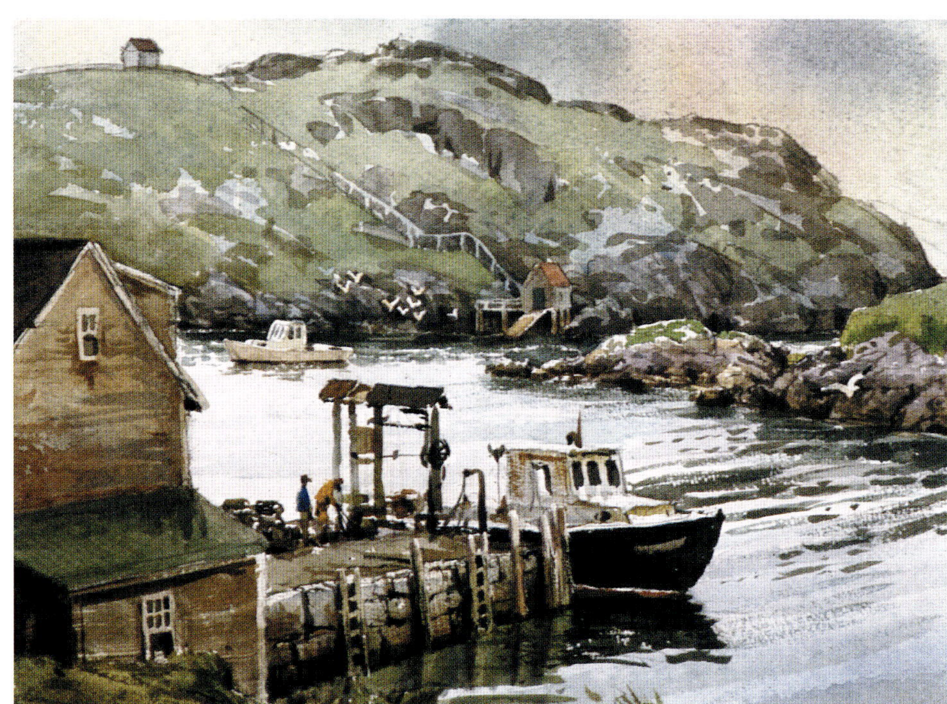

Top: Monhegan Fish House (12 x 16)
Right: Unloading, Monhegan (11 x 14)

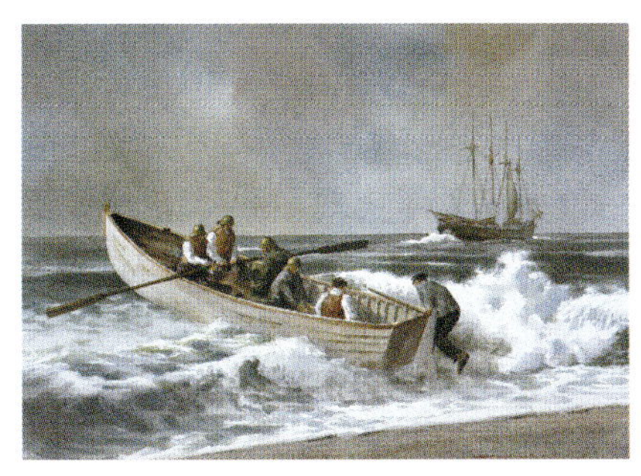

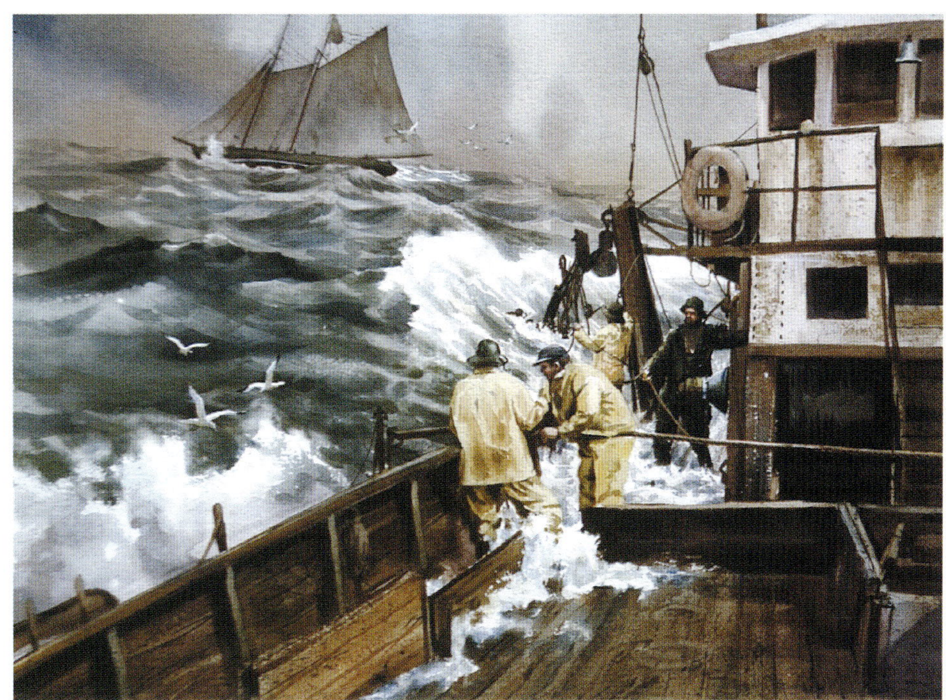

Top: Rescue Squad (16 x 20)
Right: All in a Day's Work (18 x 24)

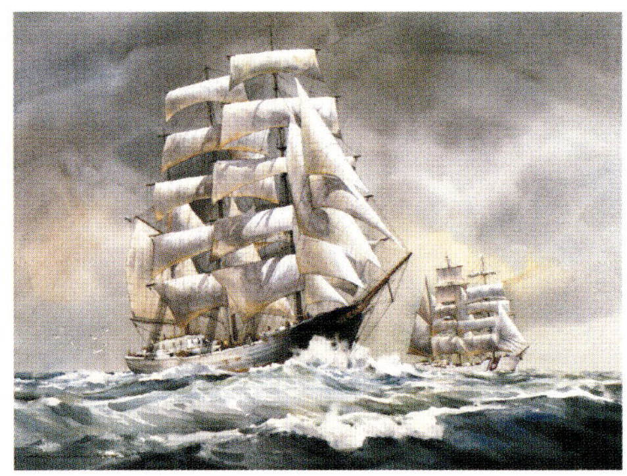

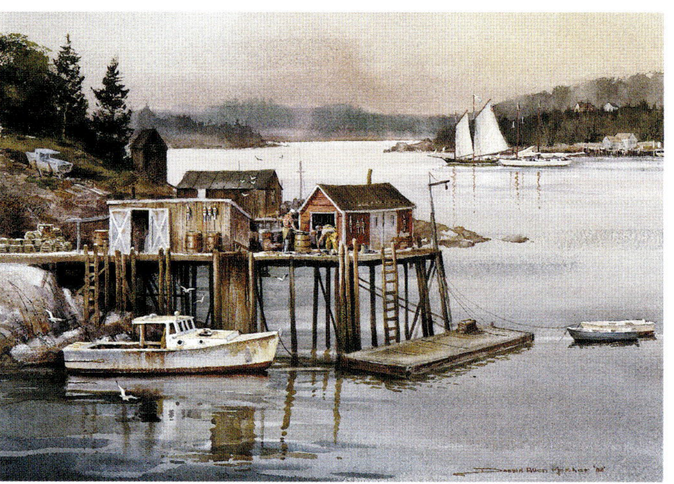

Left: Soaring with the Eagle (22 x 28)
Right: Swanns Island (10 x 12)

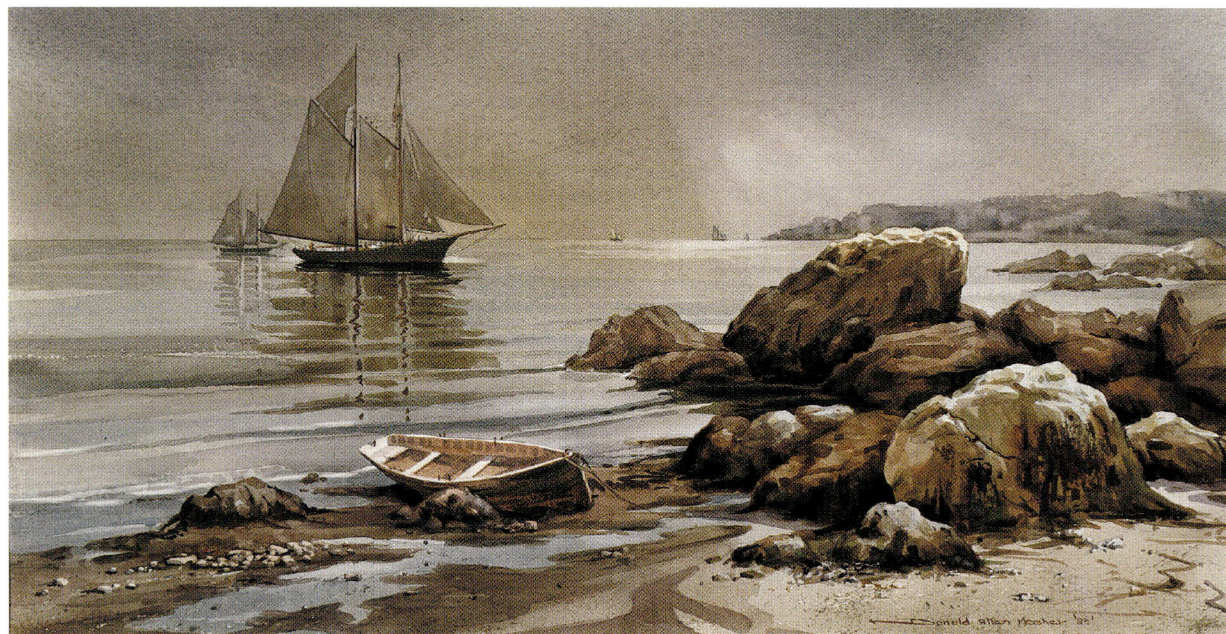

Waiting for the Tide (12 x 22)

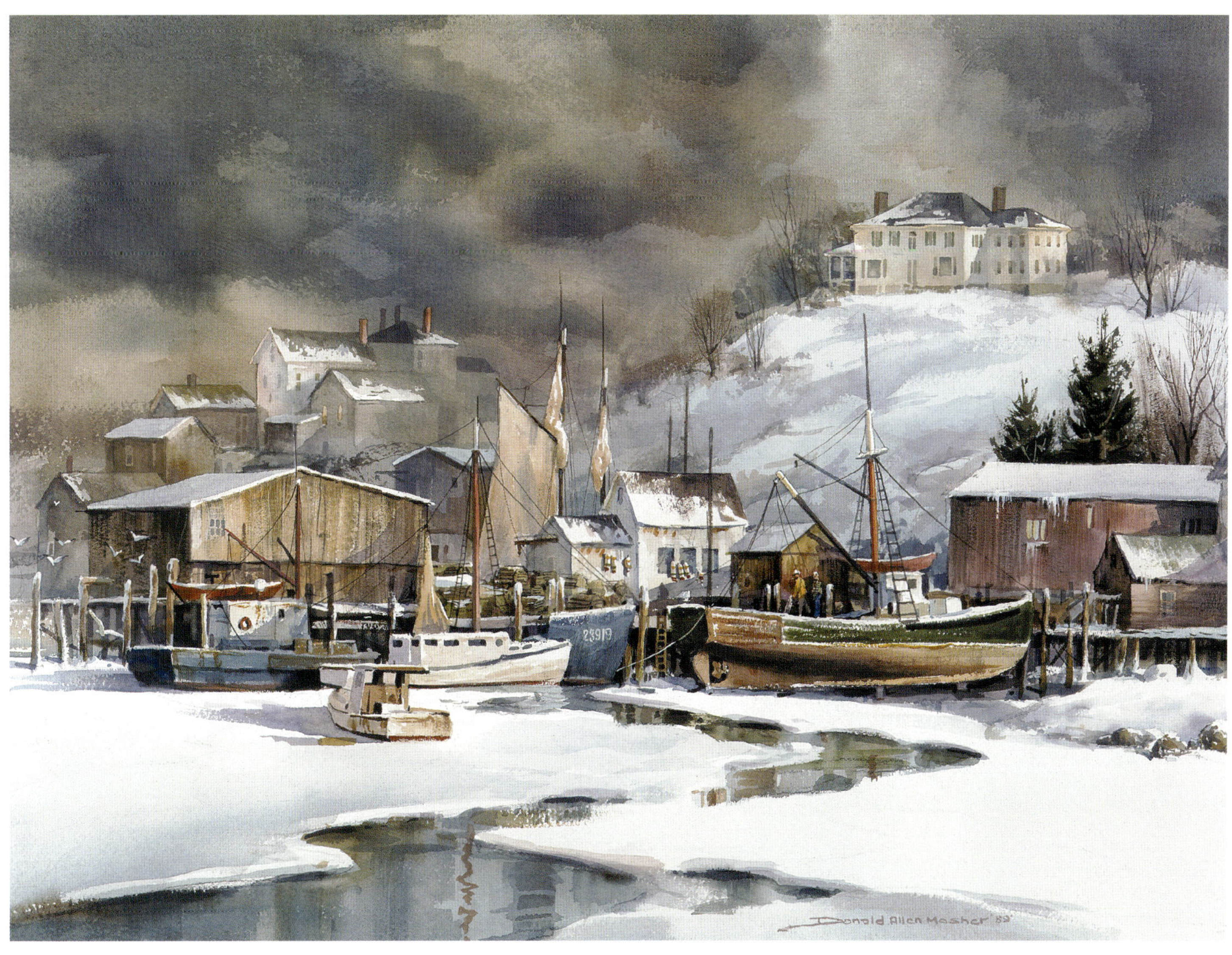

East Gloucester, Winter (22 x 30)

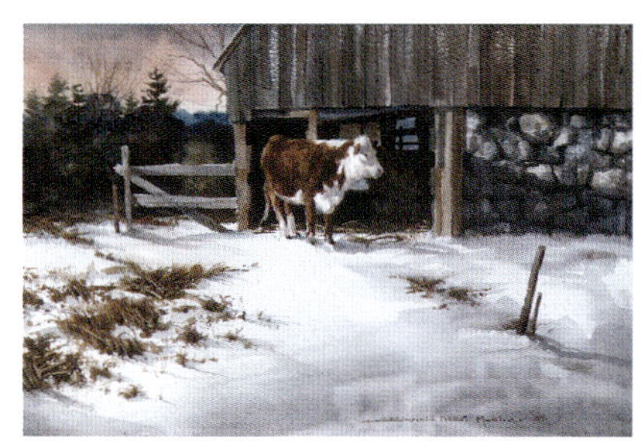

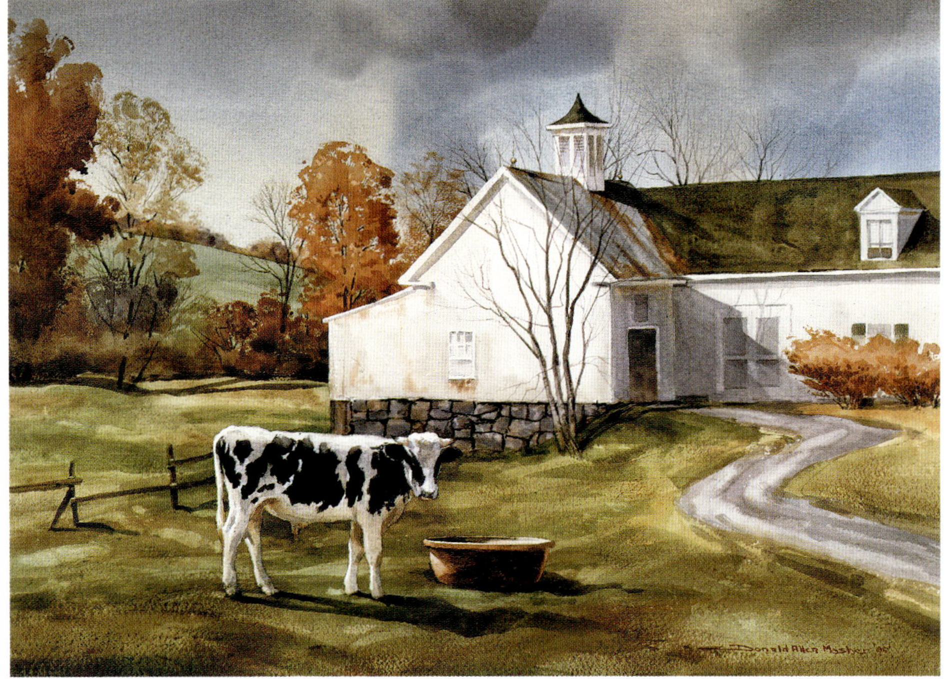

The first virtue of a painting is to be a feast for the eyes.

—Eugene Delacroix

Top: Solitude (8 x 10)
Bottom: The Visitor (15 x 26)

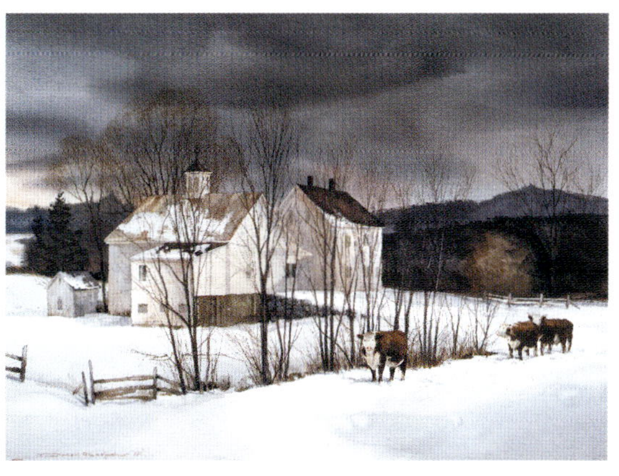

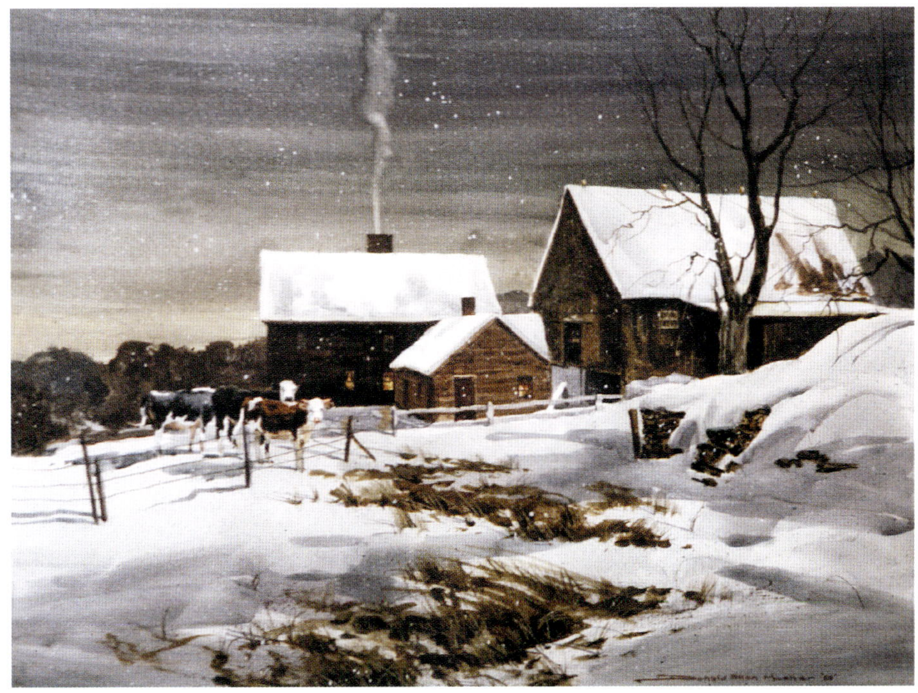

Top: March Madness (18 x 22)
Bottom: Winter Coats, New Hampshire
(20 x 30)

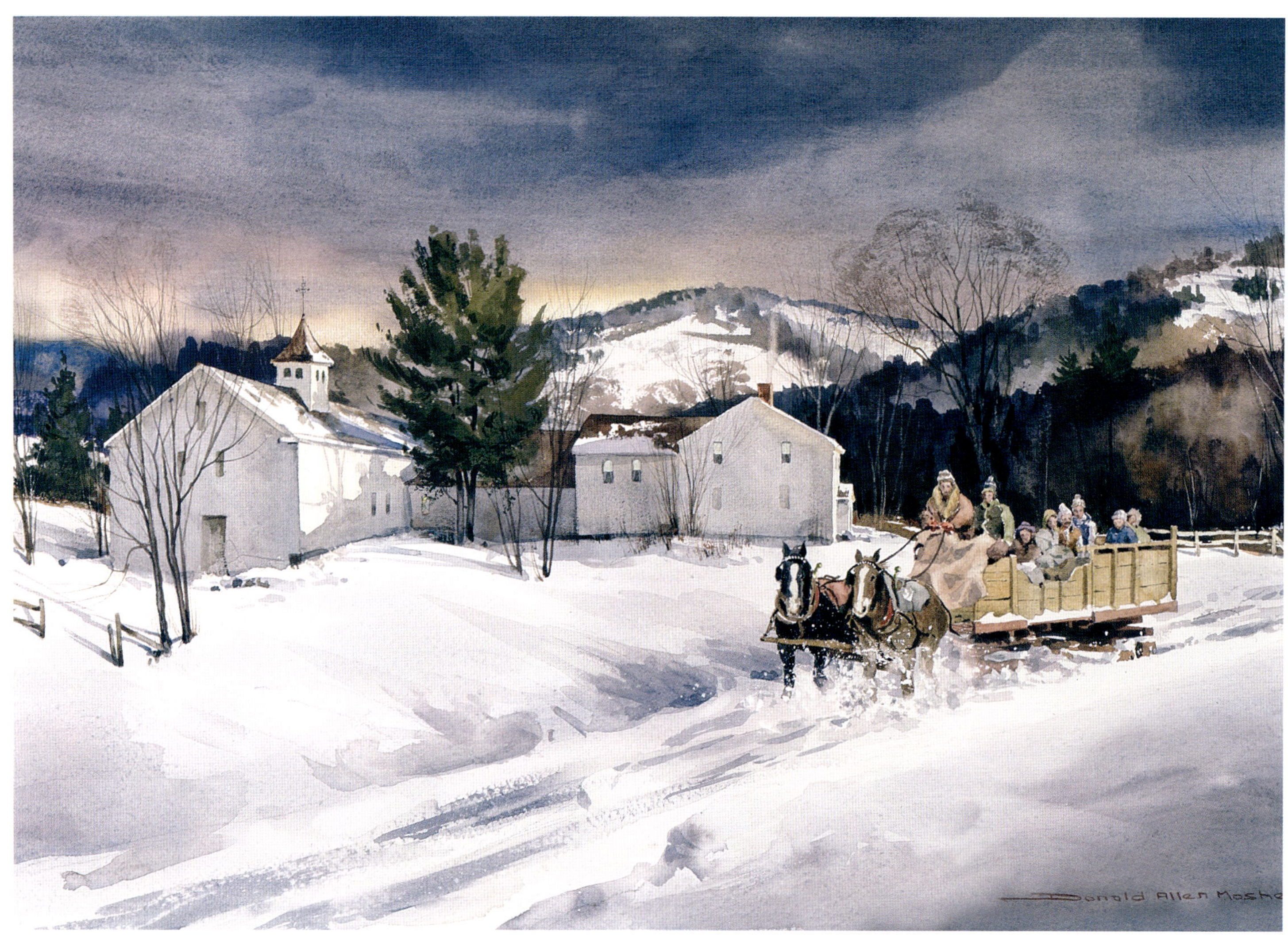

Sleigh Bells Ring (20 x 30)

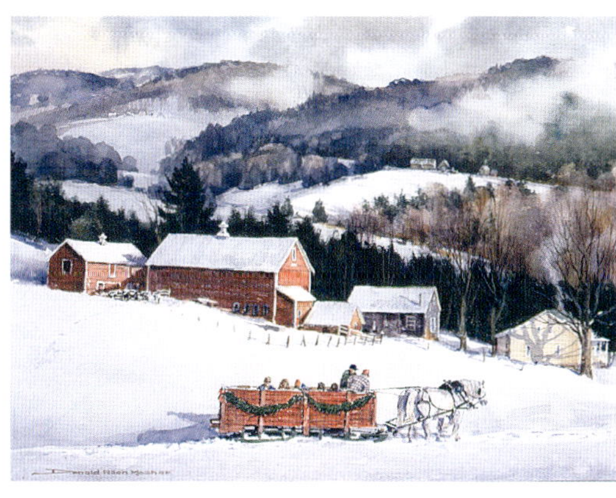

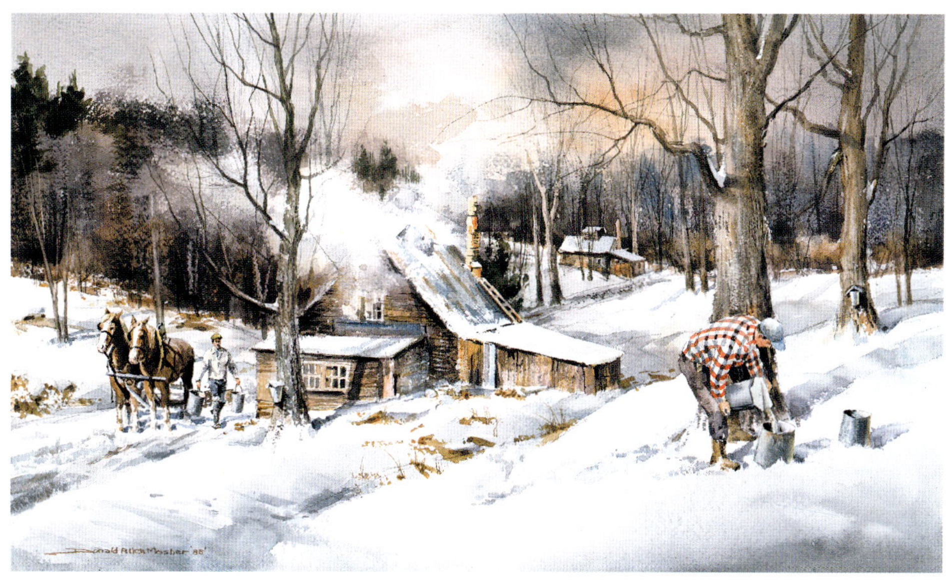

Top: Road to Stowe (18 x 26)
Bottom: Sugar Time (16 x 24)

SPRING

To be alive, to be able to see, to walk, to have music, paintings—it's all a miracle.
—Arthur Rubinstein

One day in 1990, I was sitting thinking about some of the artists whose work I admire—Gruppe, Thieme, Hibbard, and others. Suddenly I was amazed to realize that many of the paintings I think most highly of are oils. Meanwhile, I was painting in watercolors exclusively!

I realized that I had pushed watercolors as far as I could. I wanted to try something different. I didn't dip my toe in the water, I dove in. It was not an easy transition—like someone telling you, "You're fifty years old. I want you to change from writing right-handed to writing left-handed." I had to adopt an entirely new style.

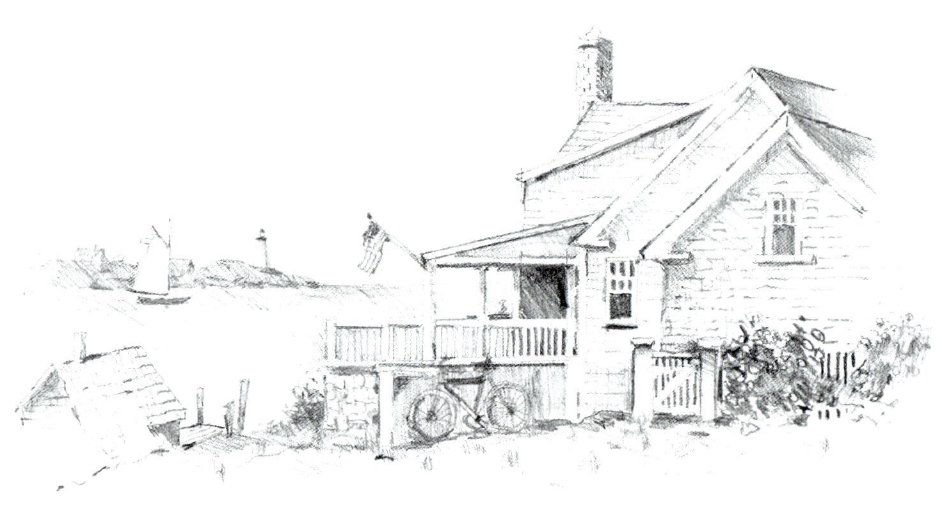

Painting in watercolors is like playing a violin, where every note has to be right; painting in oils is like playing the drums—you can bang your way through your mistakes. Watercolors require intense concentration and, for me, absolute silence. If you make a mistake, you usually have to start over. Painting in oils is less cerebral, more physical.

Spring is the season of hope. After being cooped up in my studio working on paintings started in the fall and winter, I love watching the landscape coming to life, bringing new colors to the flowers and the world around us. I usually take one or two trips to Cape Cod each spring before our gallery in Rockport gets busy. Spring roses come to life and start the cycle of the tourist season throughout New England.

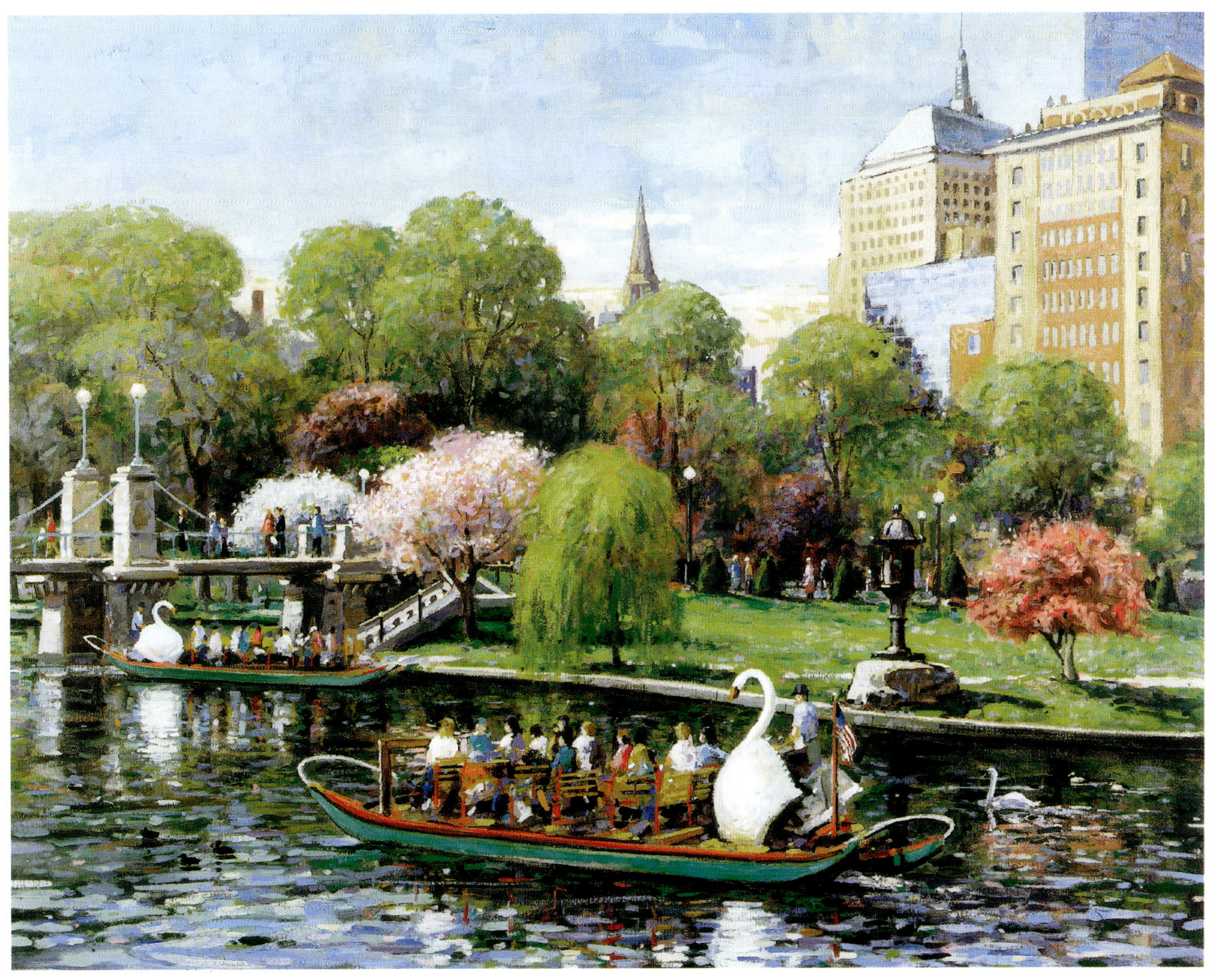

Boston Public Garden (30 x 38)

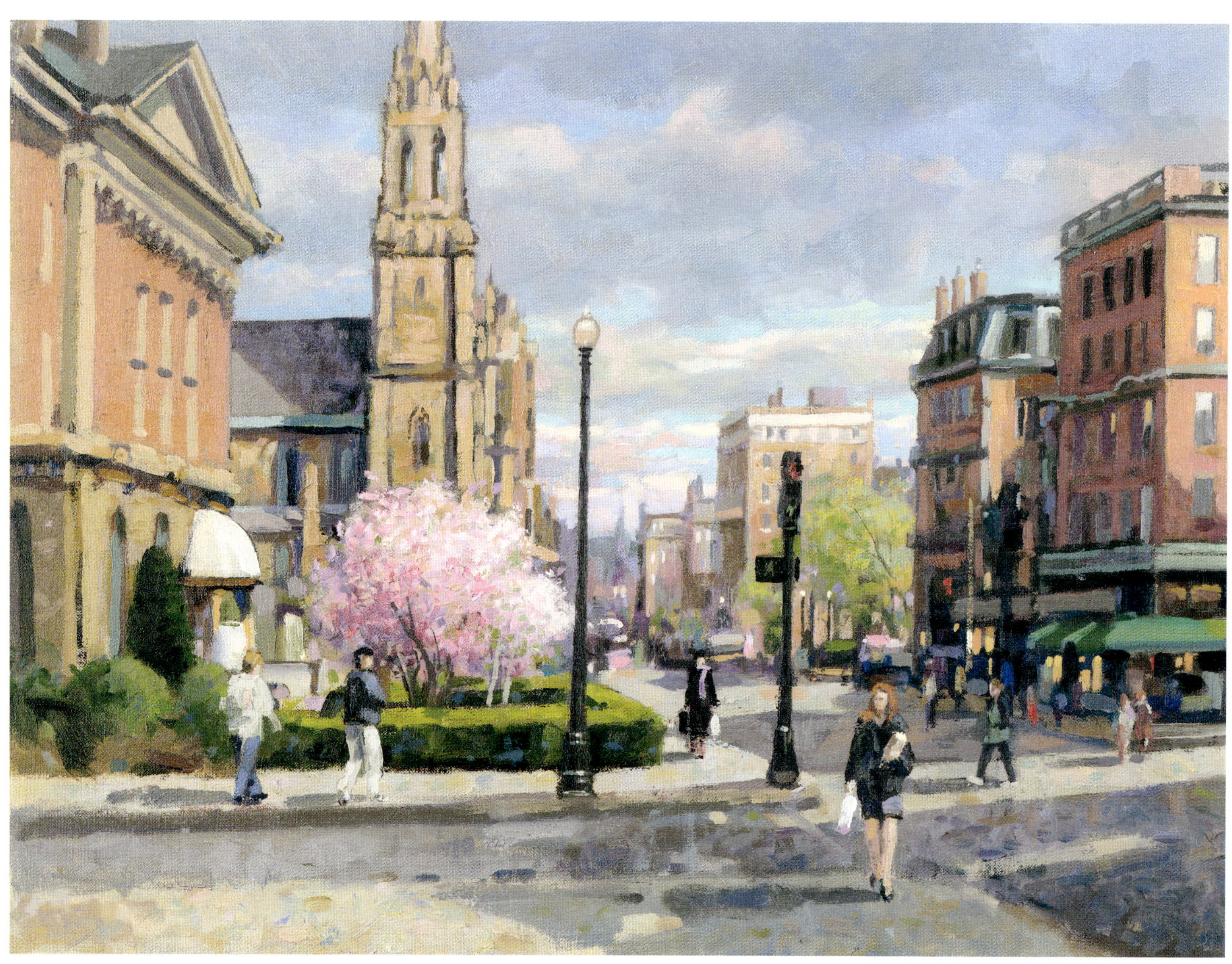

Springtime on Berkeley Street (16 x 22)

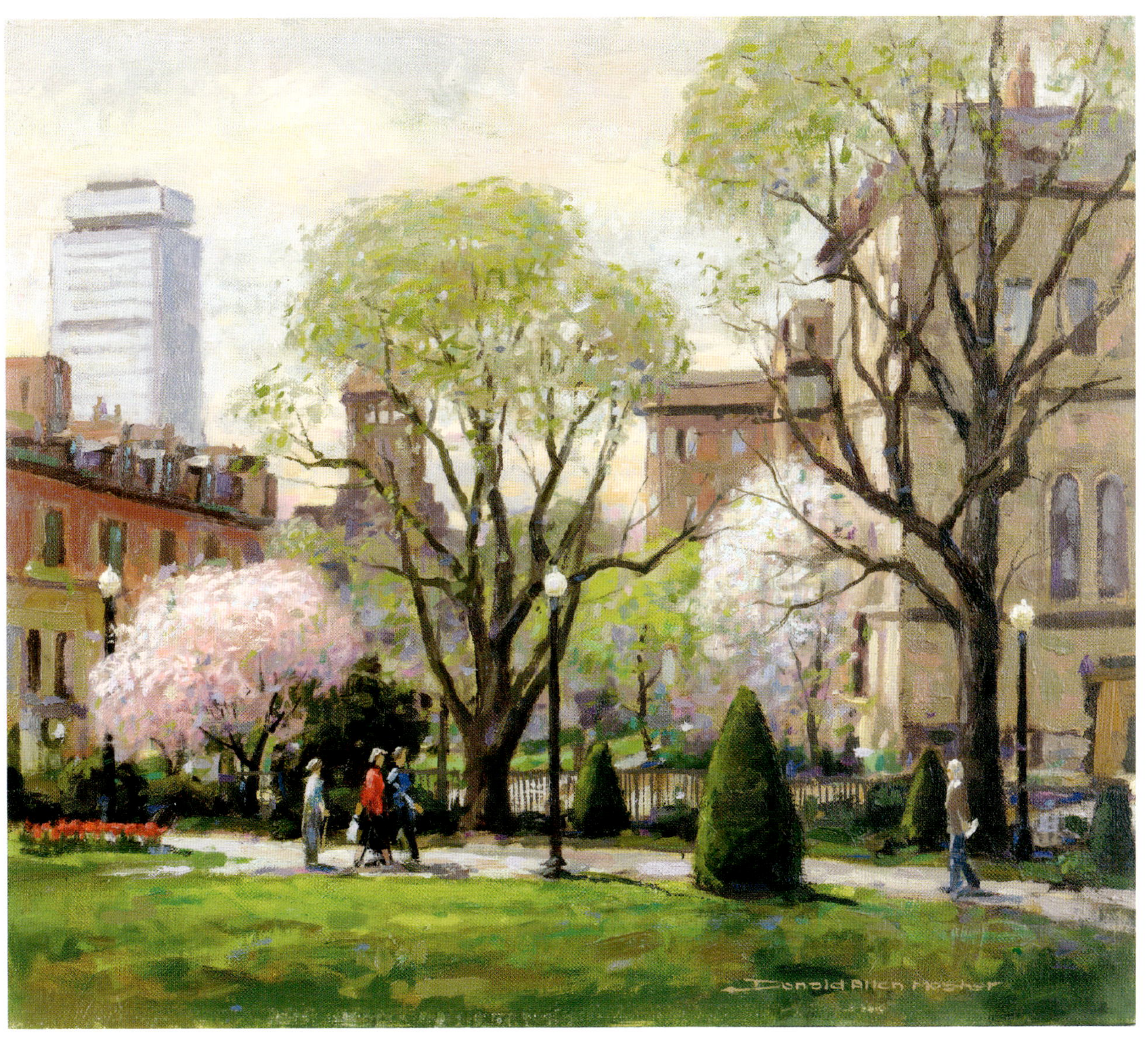

Lunch Break, Boston Public Garden (14 x 18)

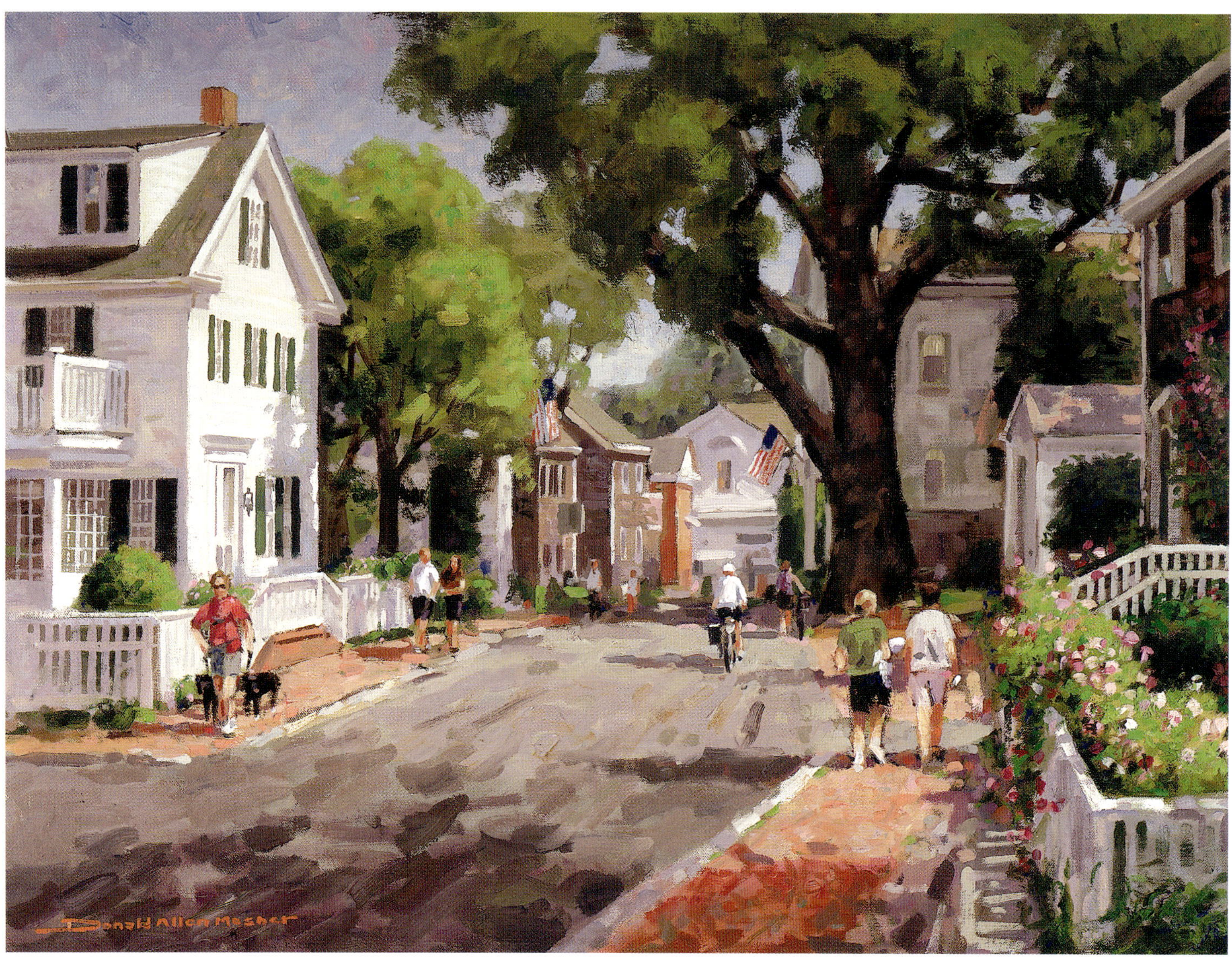

The Pagoda Tree (24 x 30)

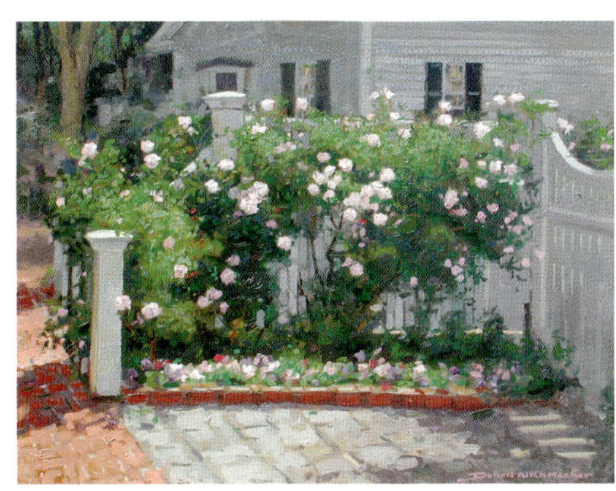

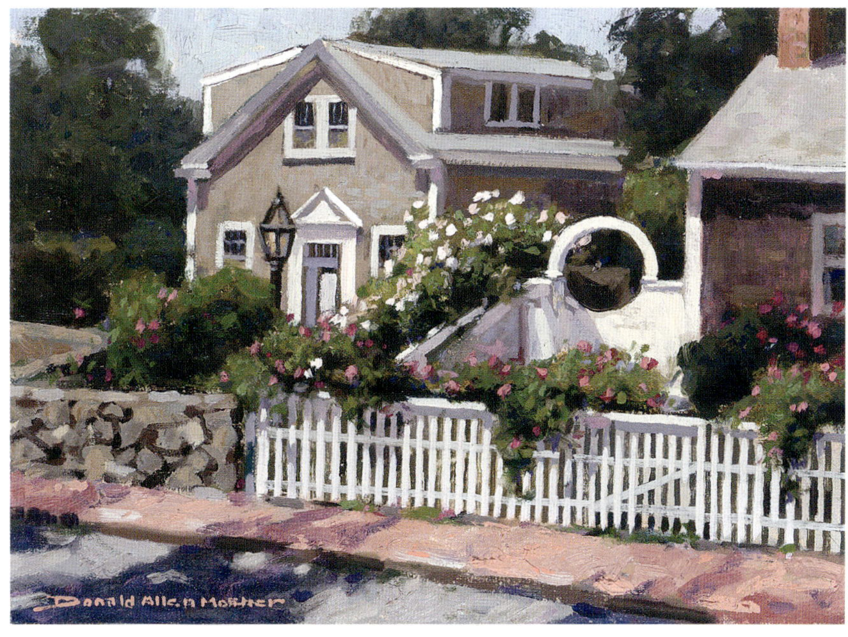

Top: Cape Roses (25 x 30)
Bottom: Spring Cottage (11 x 14)

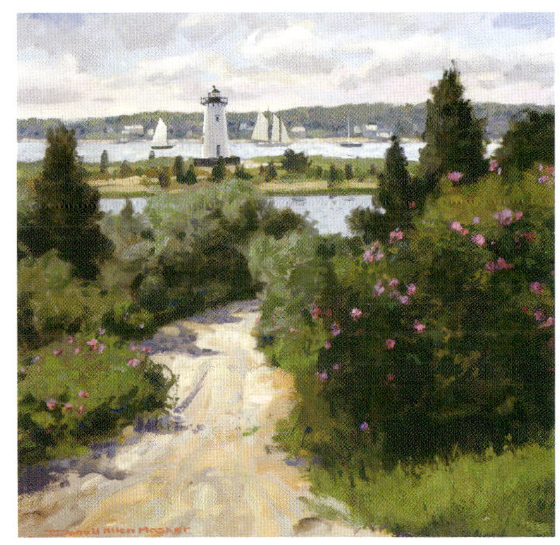

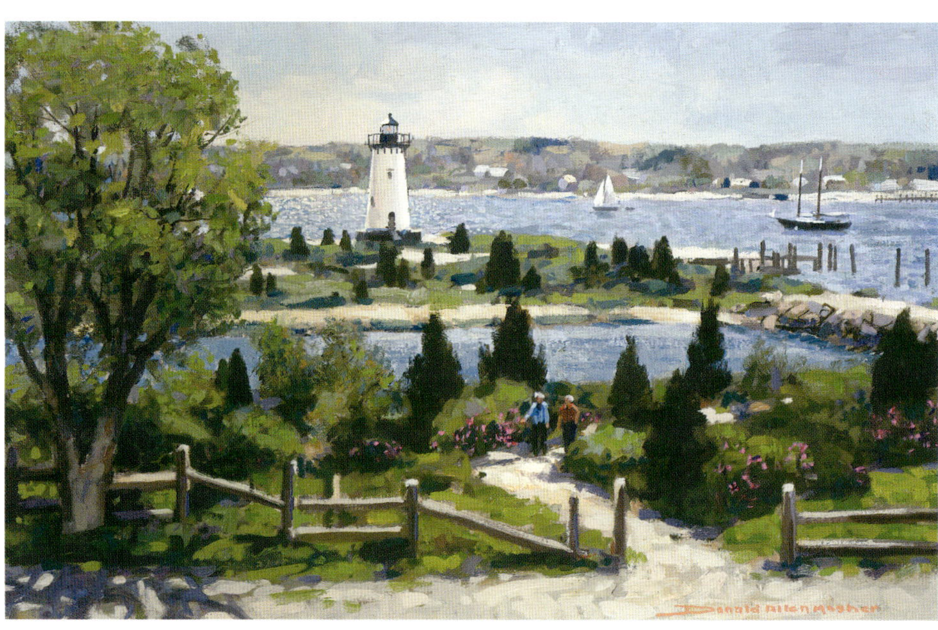

Top: Lighthouse Path (16 x 16)
Bottom: Harbor View (16 x 24)

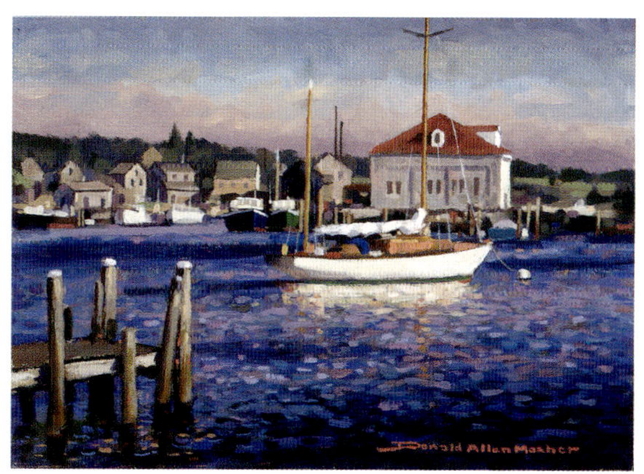

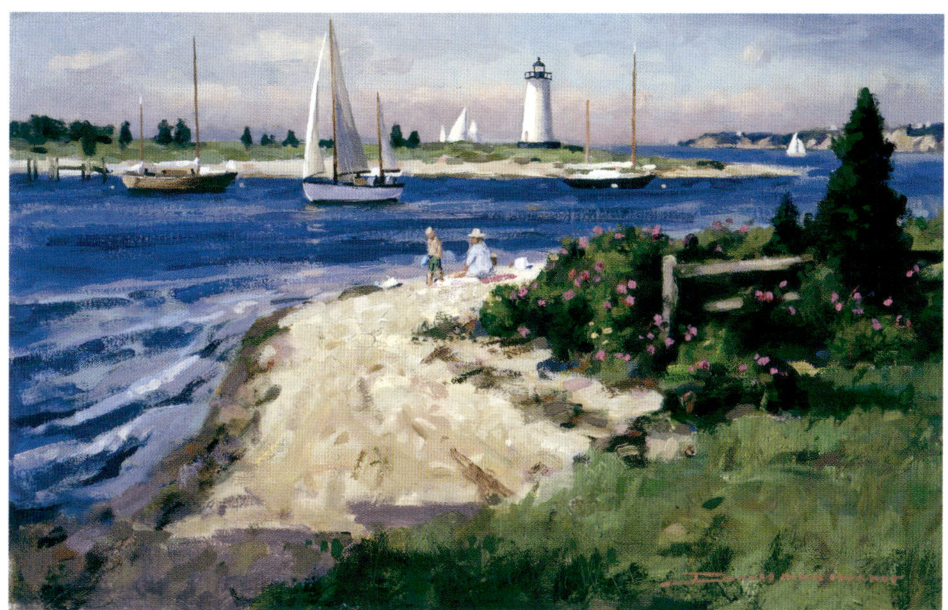

Top: Last Light, Menemsha (12 x 16)
Bottom: Waiting for the Ferry (16 x 24)

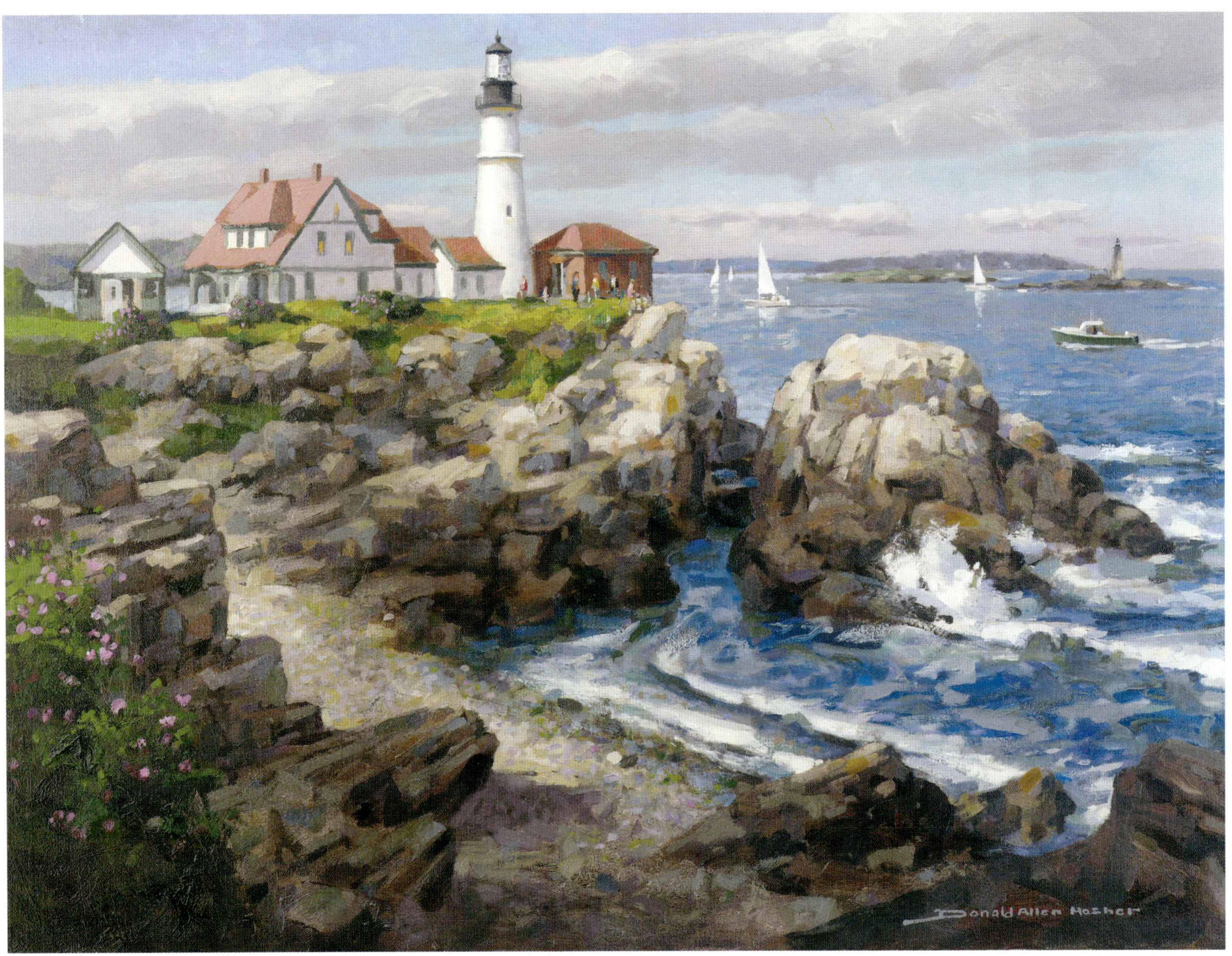

Portland Head Light (26 x 35)

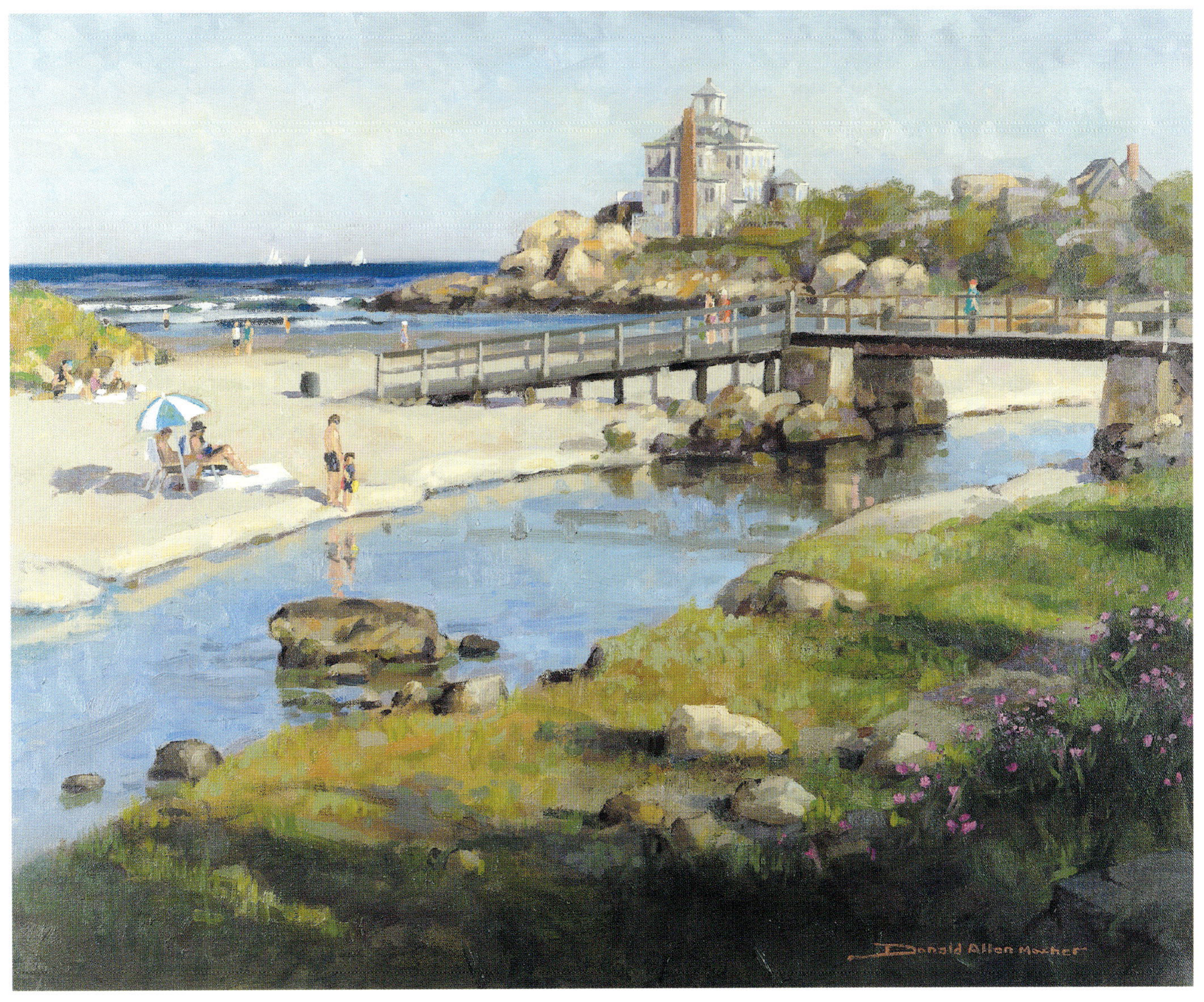

The Creek at Good Harbor (24 x 30)

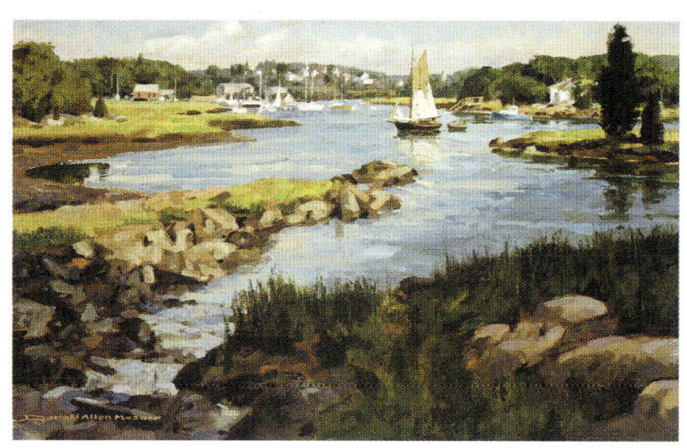

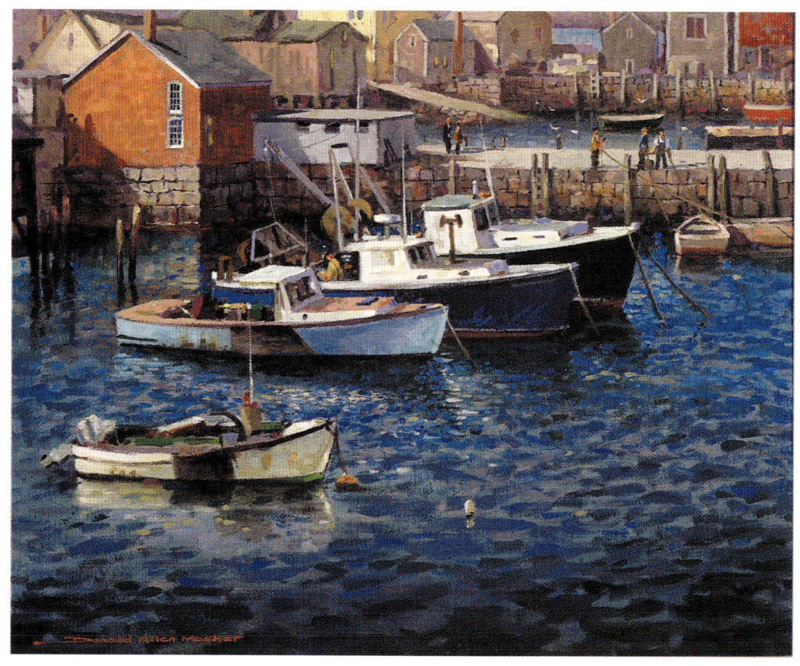

Top: Little River Sail (16 x 24)
Bottom: From the Studio (25 x 30)

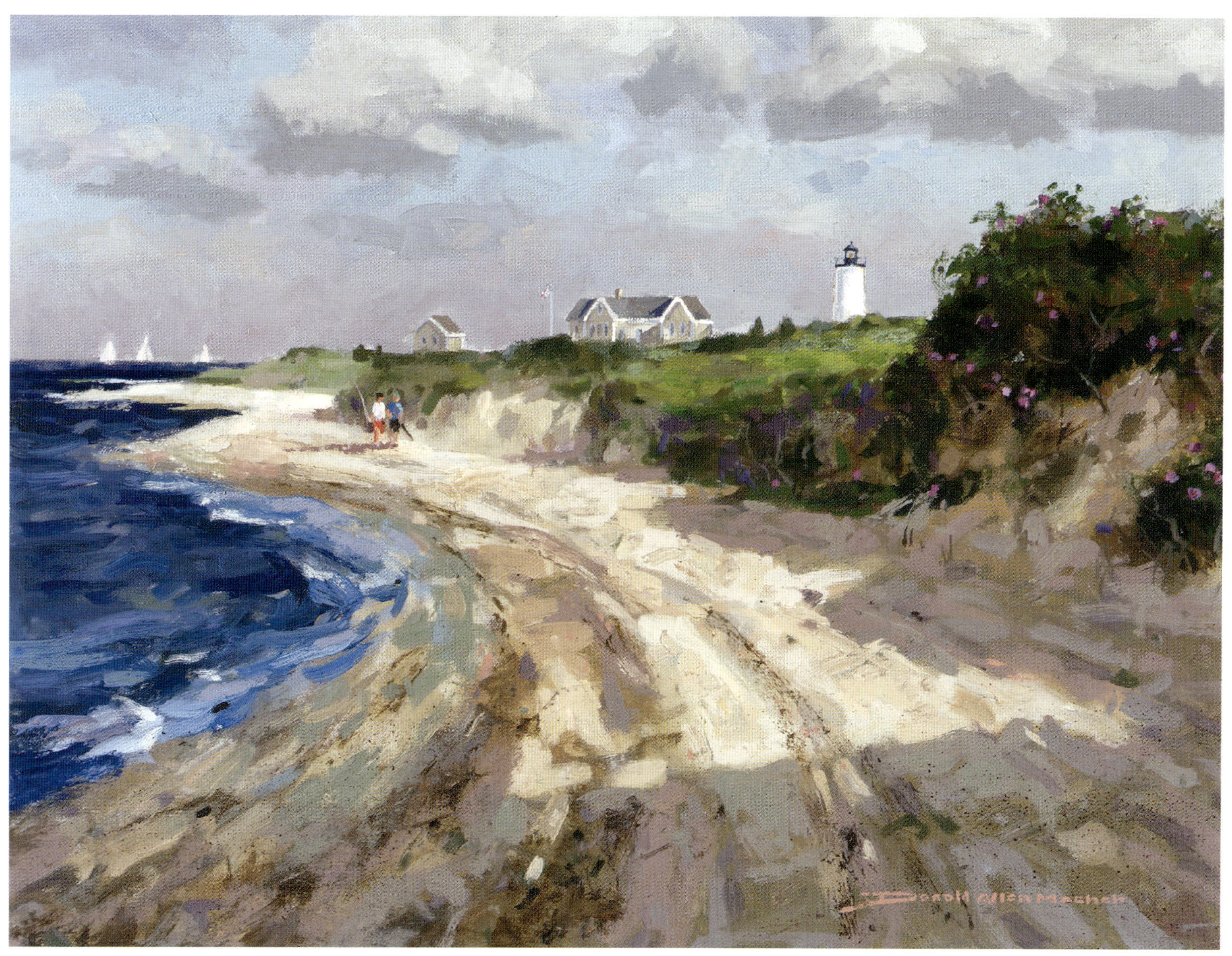

Spring Cleaning (16 x 22)

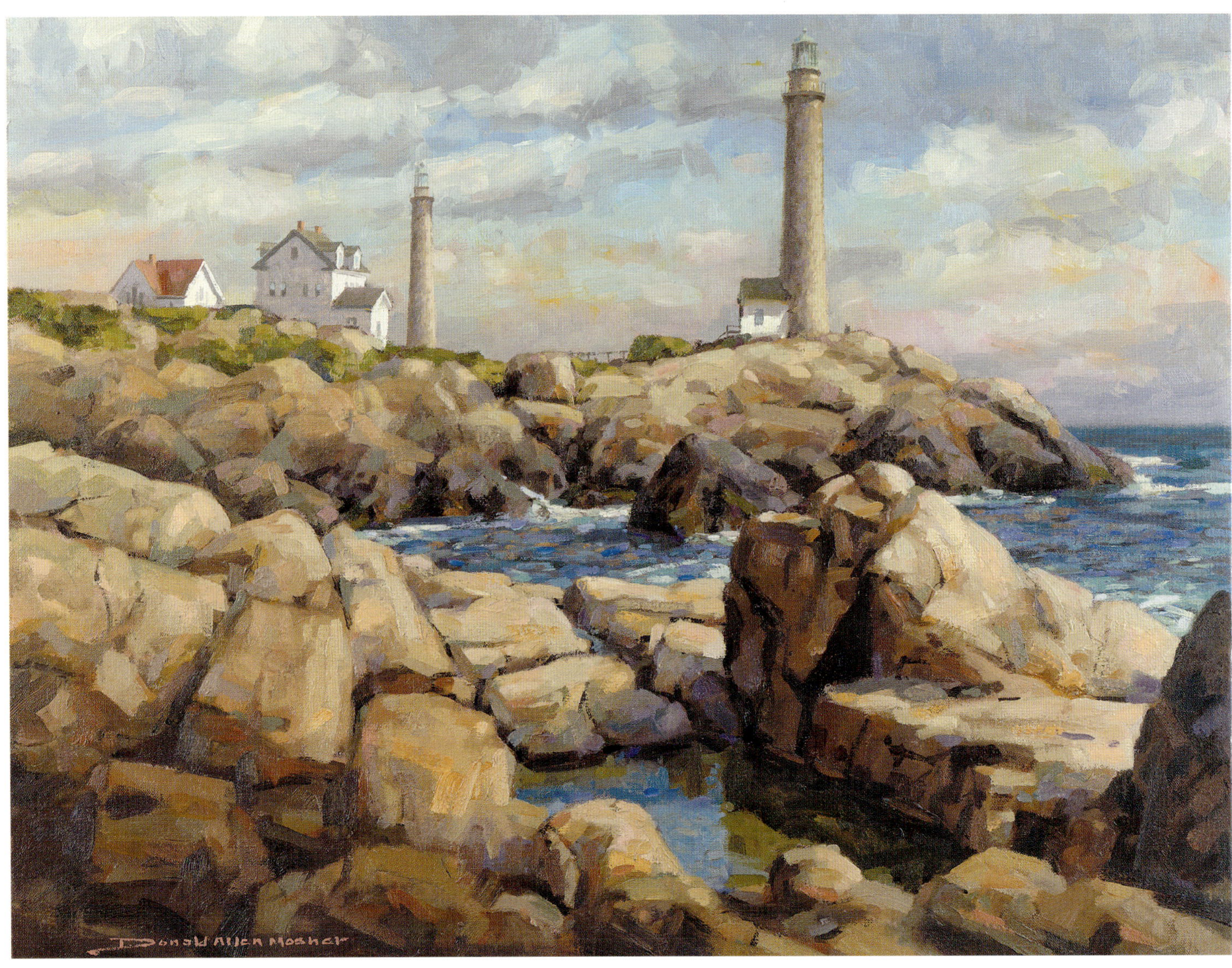

Out on Thacher Island (24 x 30)

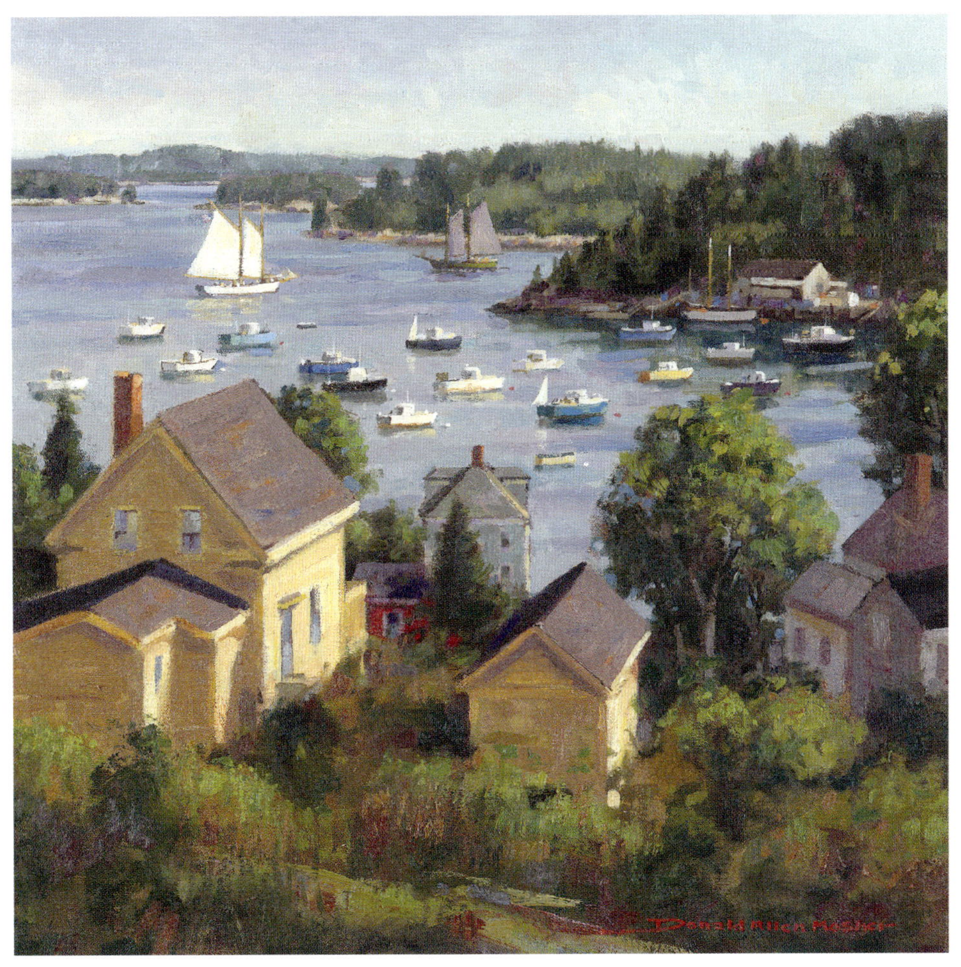

They Come and Go on Deer Island (24 x 24)

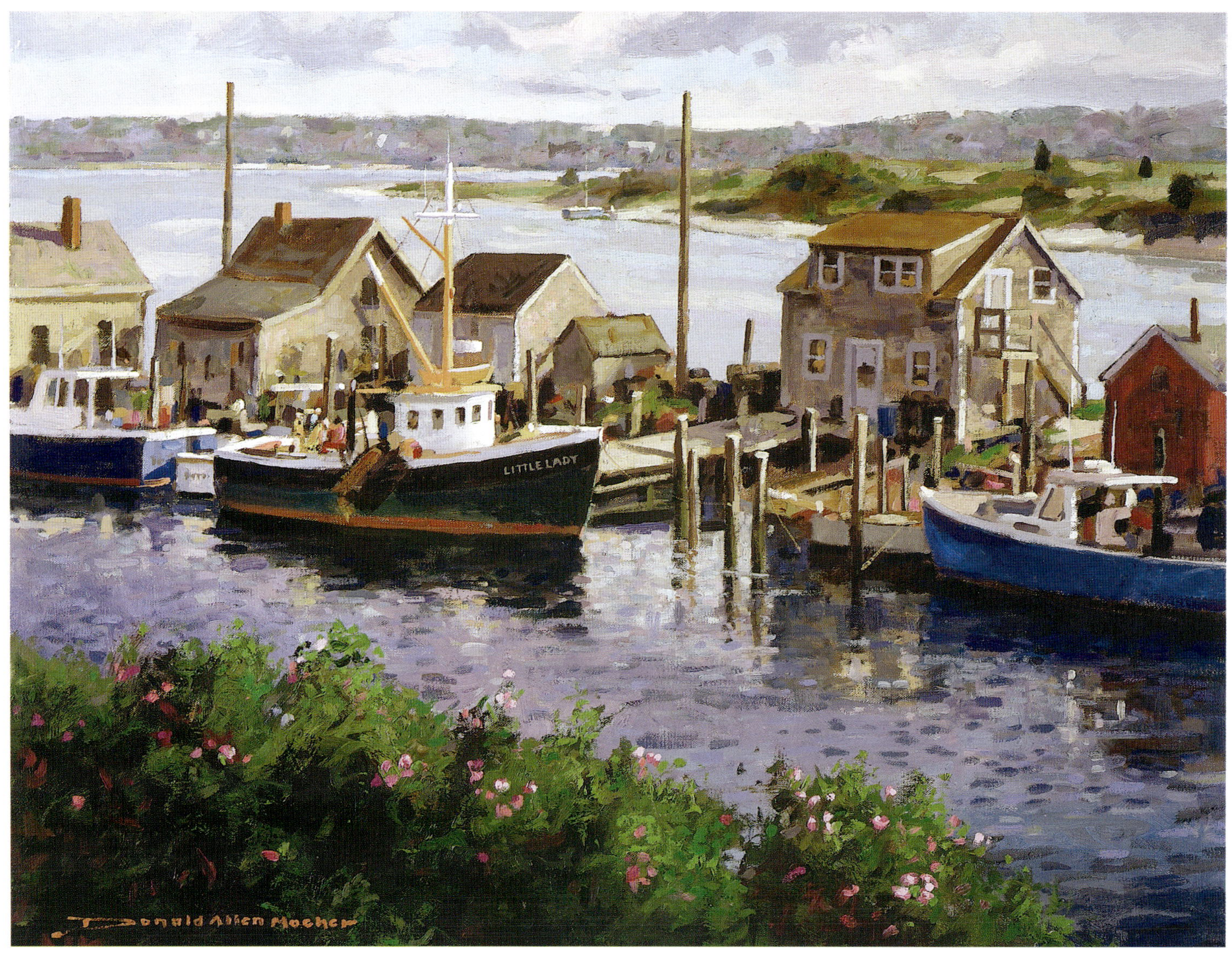

The Little Lady (24 x 30)

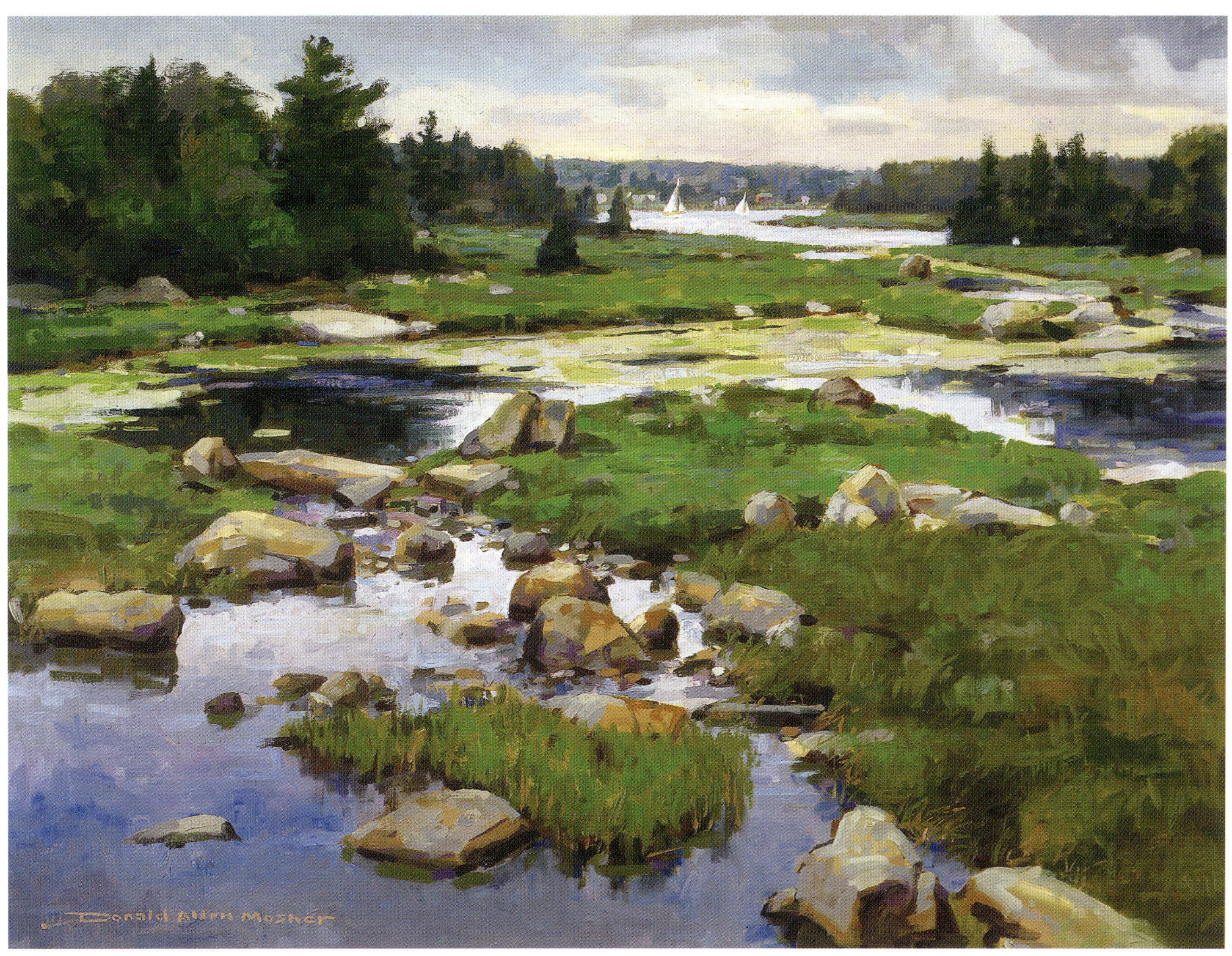

Tidal Pools, Bar Harbor (26 X 32)

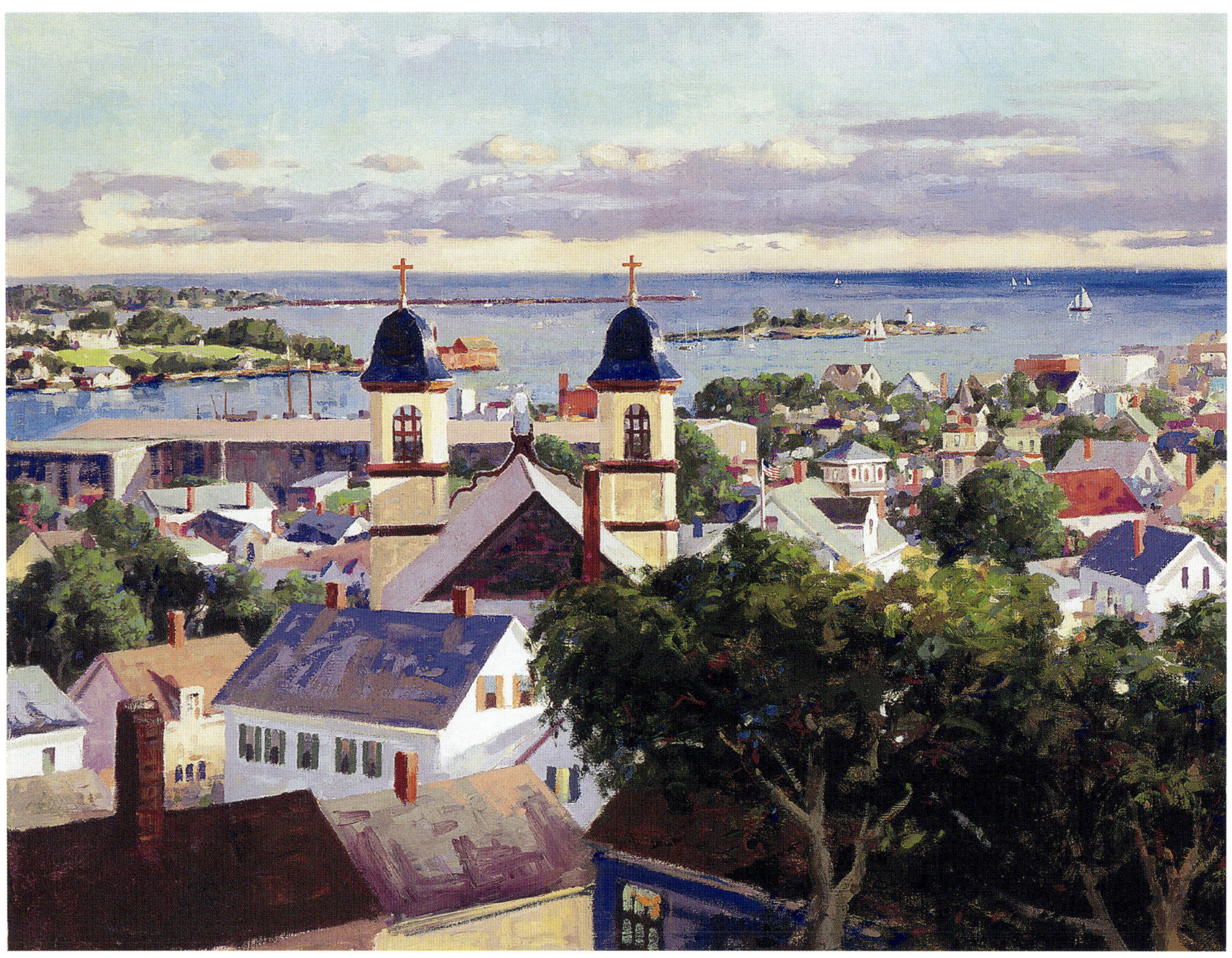

Port of Good Voyage (25 x 30)

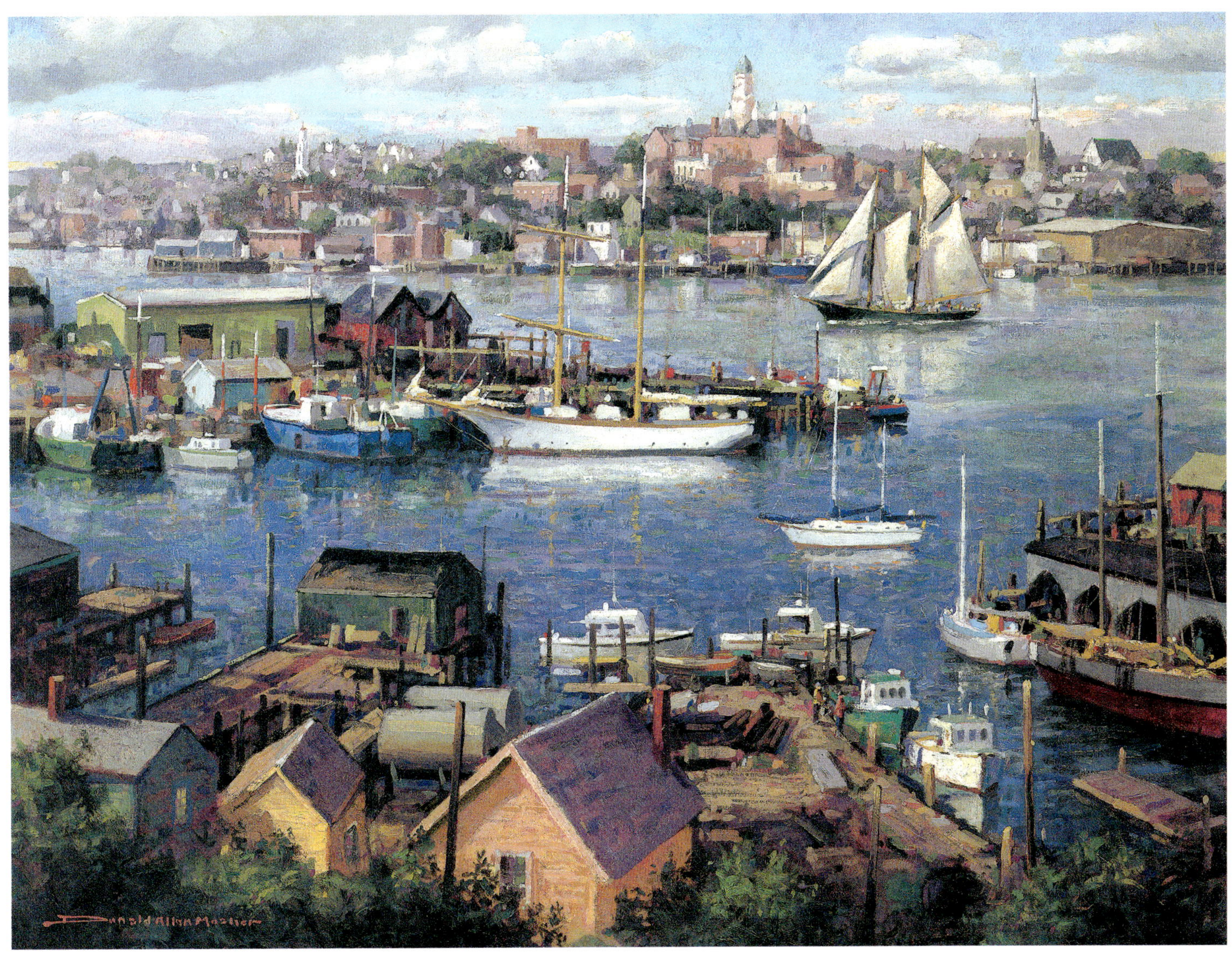

Gloucester Overlook (26 x 34)

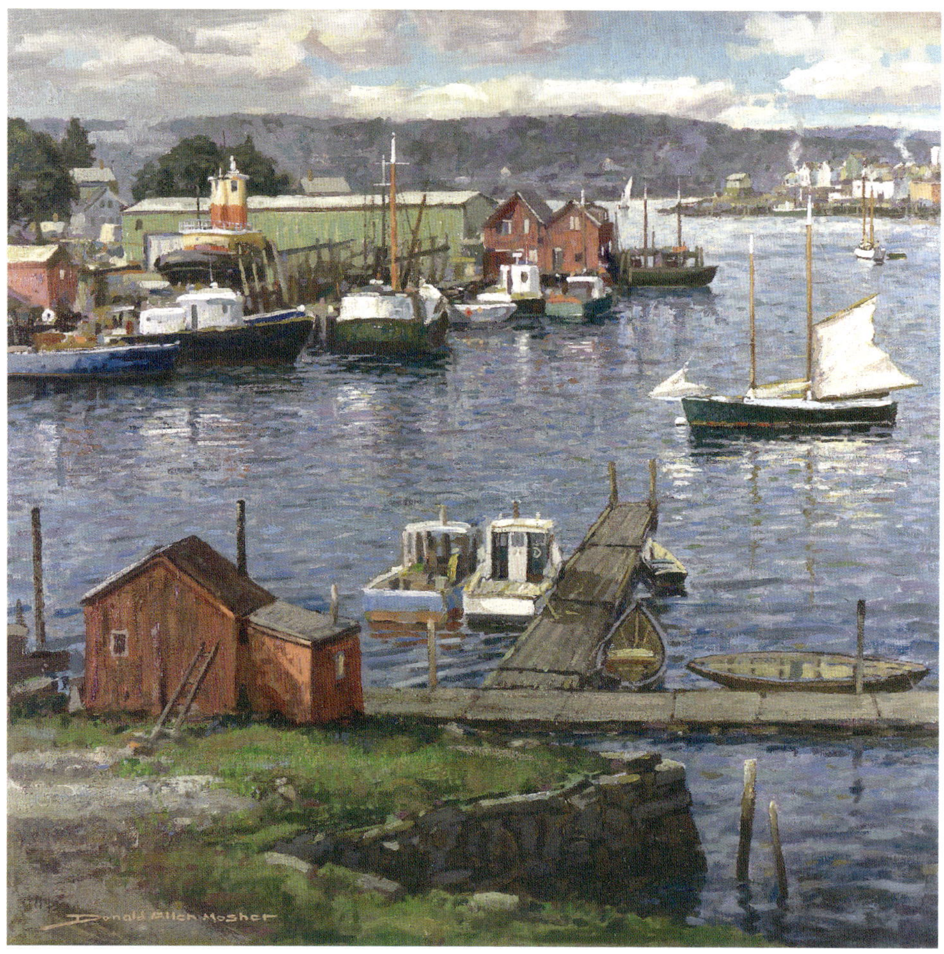

The true artist works in great gusts of effort, and in small gusts of apparent lassitude. He is not lying about "waiting for some inspiration." He is in the travail of the dreamer entering into expression.

—John F. Carlson

Ready for Spring, Gloucester (36 x 36)

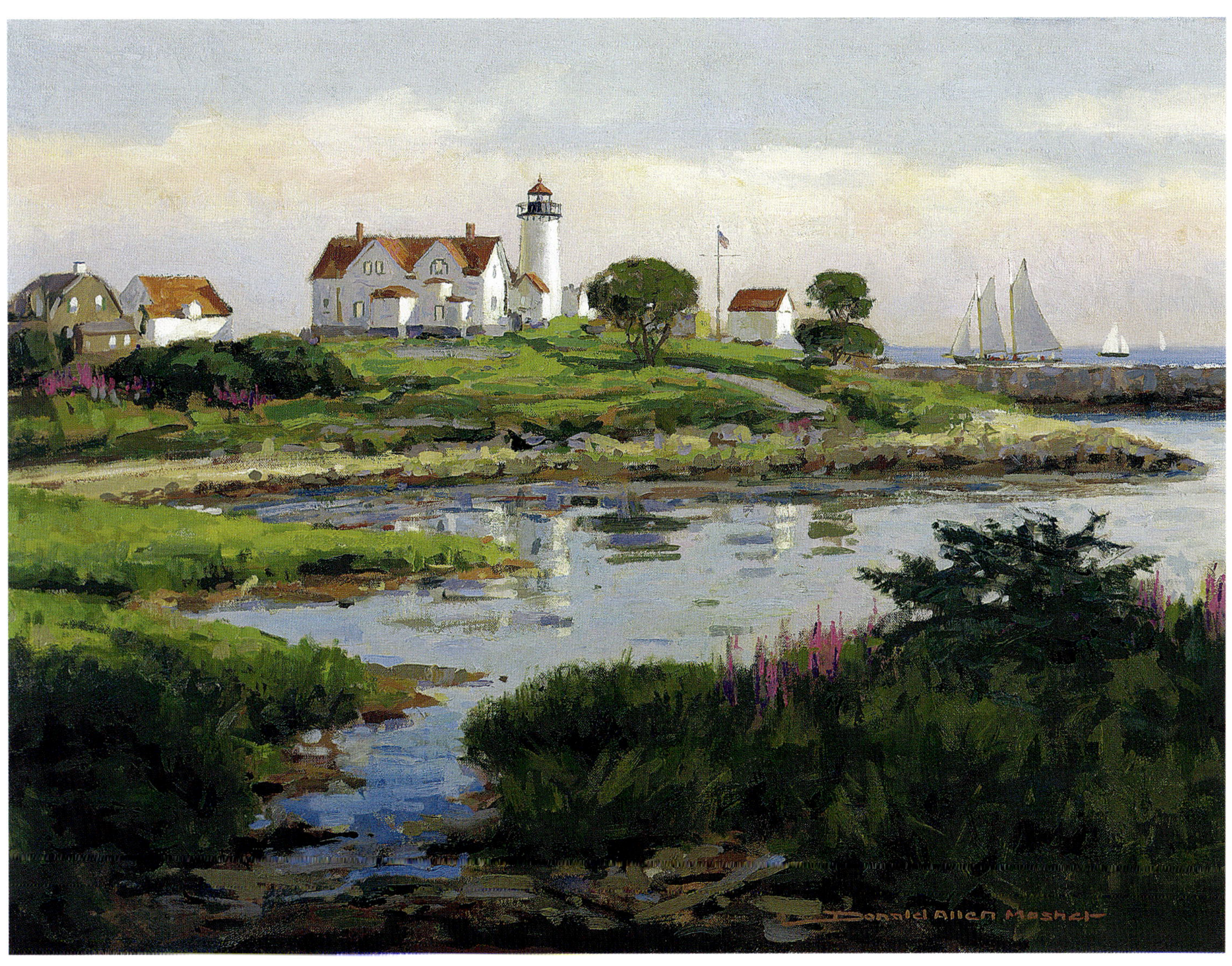

Eastern Point Lighthouse (24 x 30)

SUMMER

Time is holding its breath for an instant and for all eternity. That's what I am after.
—Andrew Wyeth

We in the Northeast may especially enjoy the warm months because of the harsh winters we endure. Summer is the busiest season in New England. Tourists fill the villages and coastal towns from southern Connecticut to the northern tips of Vermont, New Hampshire, and Maine. Rockport, where I live, is no different. I enjoy seeing the harbor filled with lobster boats and sailing vessels; I love the smell of fresh seafood cooking in the air. I don't travel as much in the summer, except for day trips to Boston and southern Maine. I spend a lot of time painting the beaches and street scenes. The many shades of green are quite a challenge.

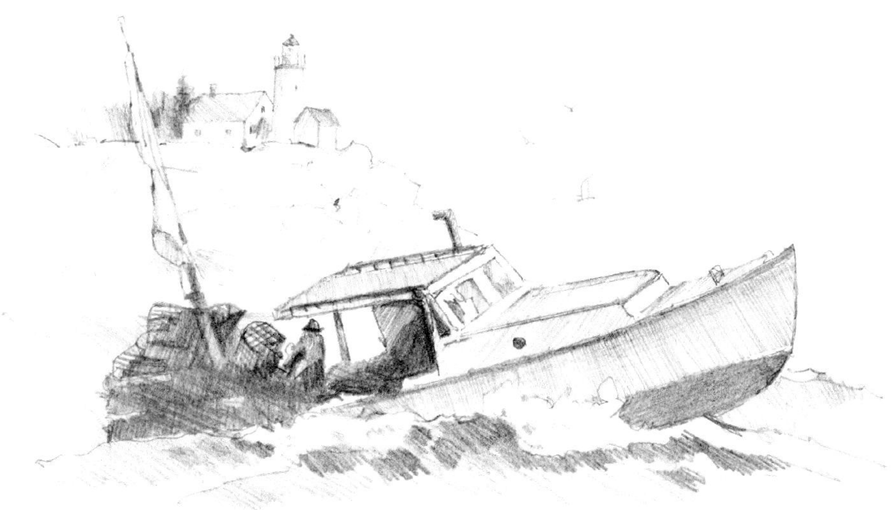

Summer is also the time for the golf course. It's a beautiful place not only to observe nature but also to clear the mind. Golf and painting are similar; both are magically frustrating. In both, you constantly struggle to improve while being held back by your own limitations.

I like to go on location and start a painting outside, then go back to the same location at least two or three times at the same time of day on a similar day. I then take photographs and finish the painting in my studio. It can take anywhere from ten to fifty hours in the studio to finish a work.

I don't start as many paintings on a trip as I once did. Instead of starting ten canvases, I'll start only three and return to them several times while I'm on location. I have over a hundred starts in my studio that I haven't completed. Some I'll take up next year and work on again. Some I may never finish. I have one friend who doesn't want me to finish any of them, just sign them. He says they look good the way they are.

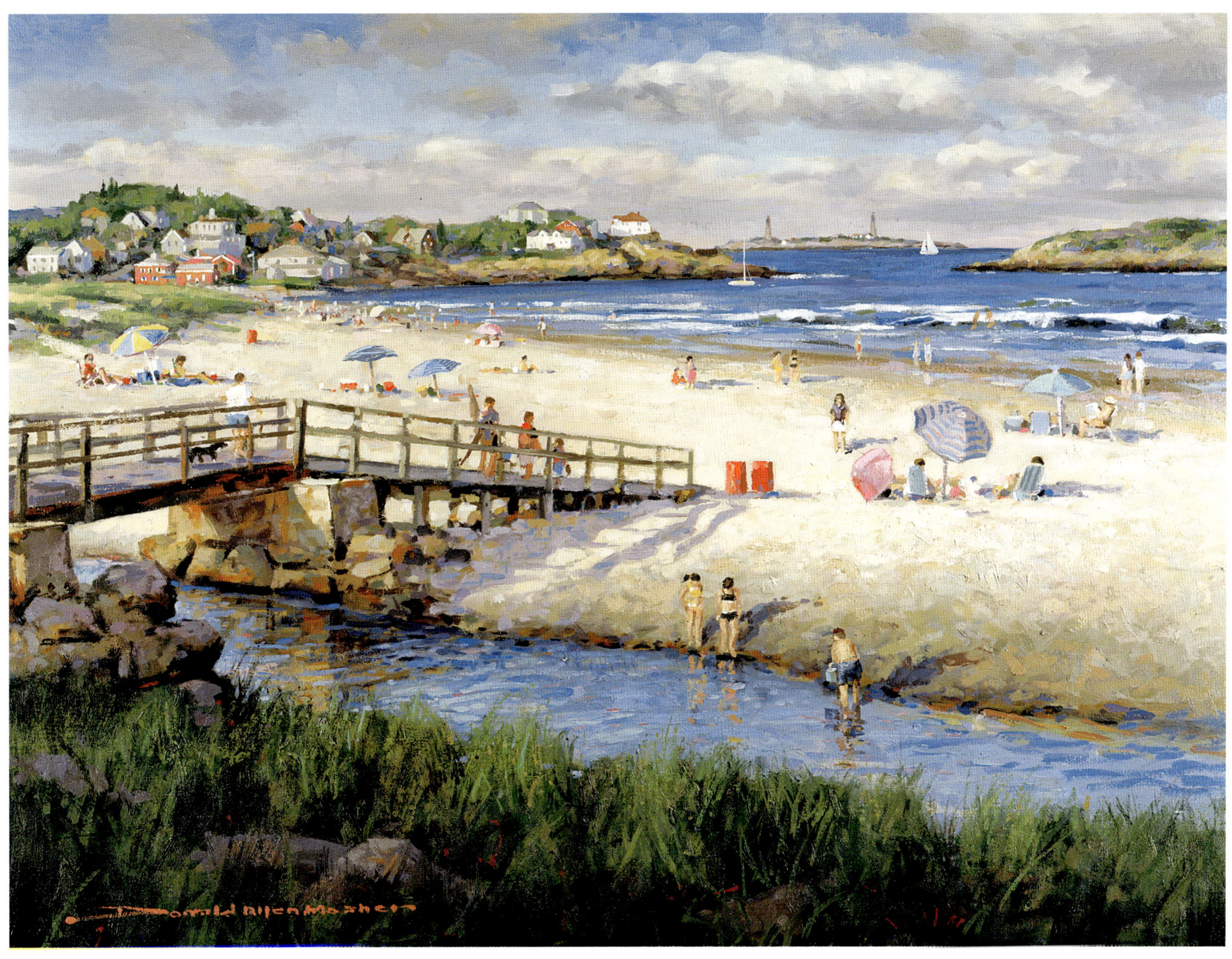

Good Harbor Beach (30 x 36)

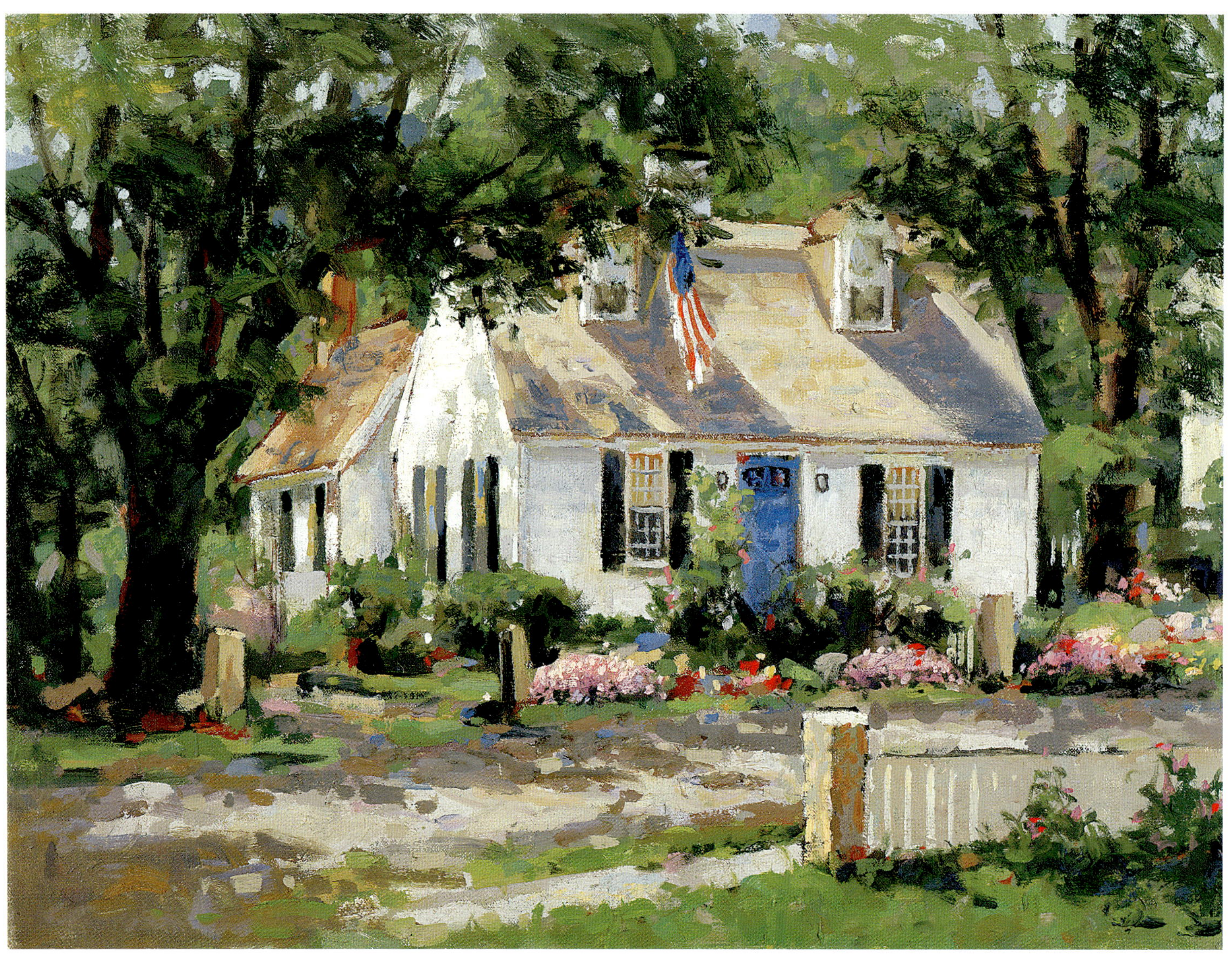

Independence Day (16 x 22)

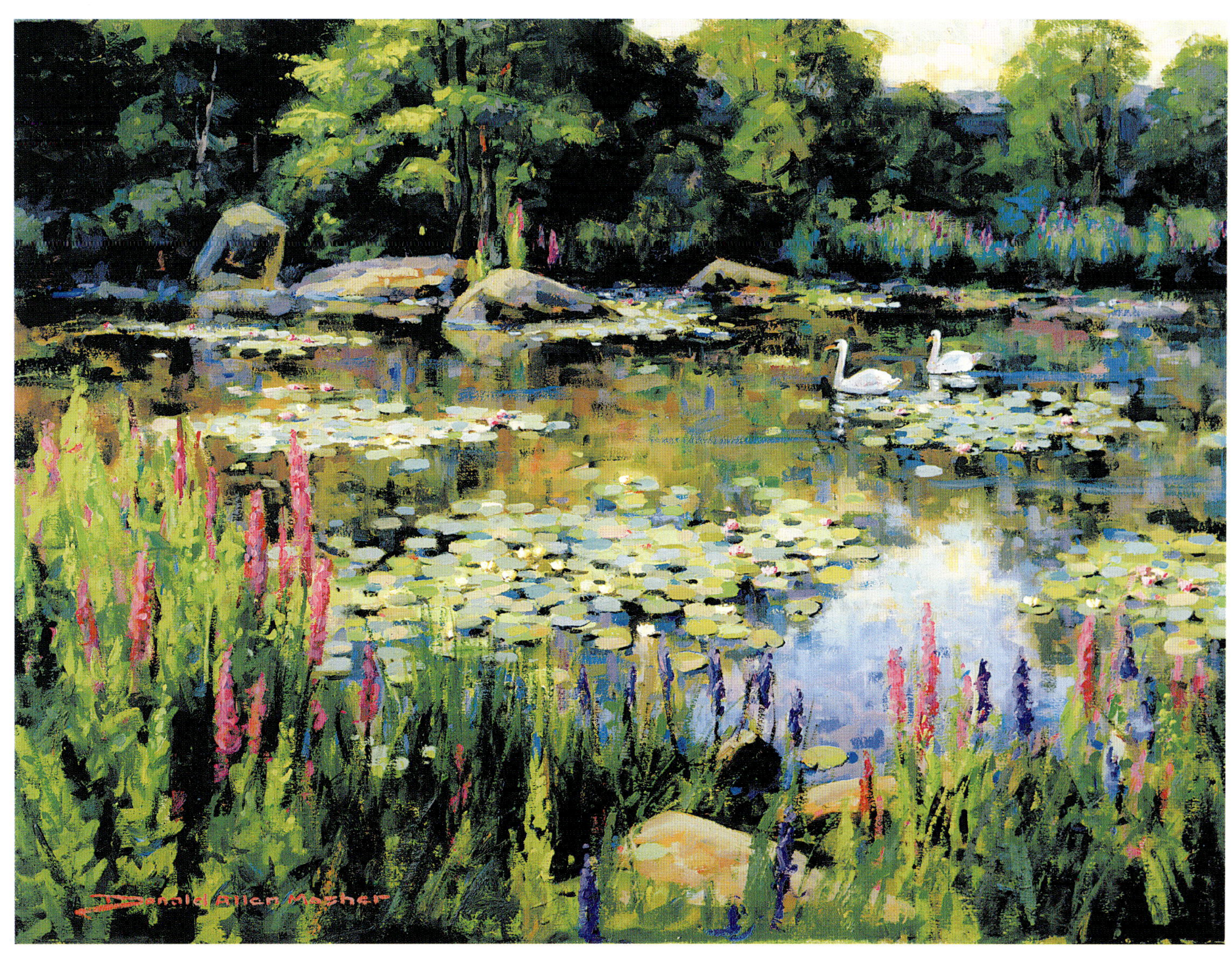

The Lily Pond (22 x 28)

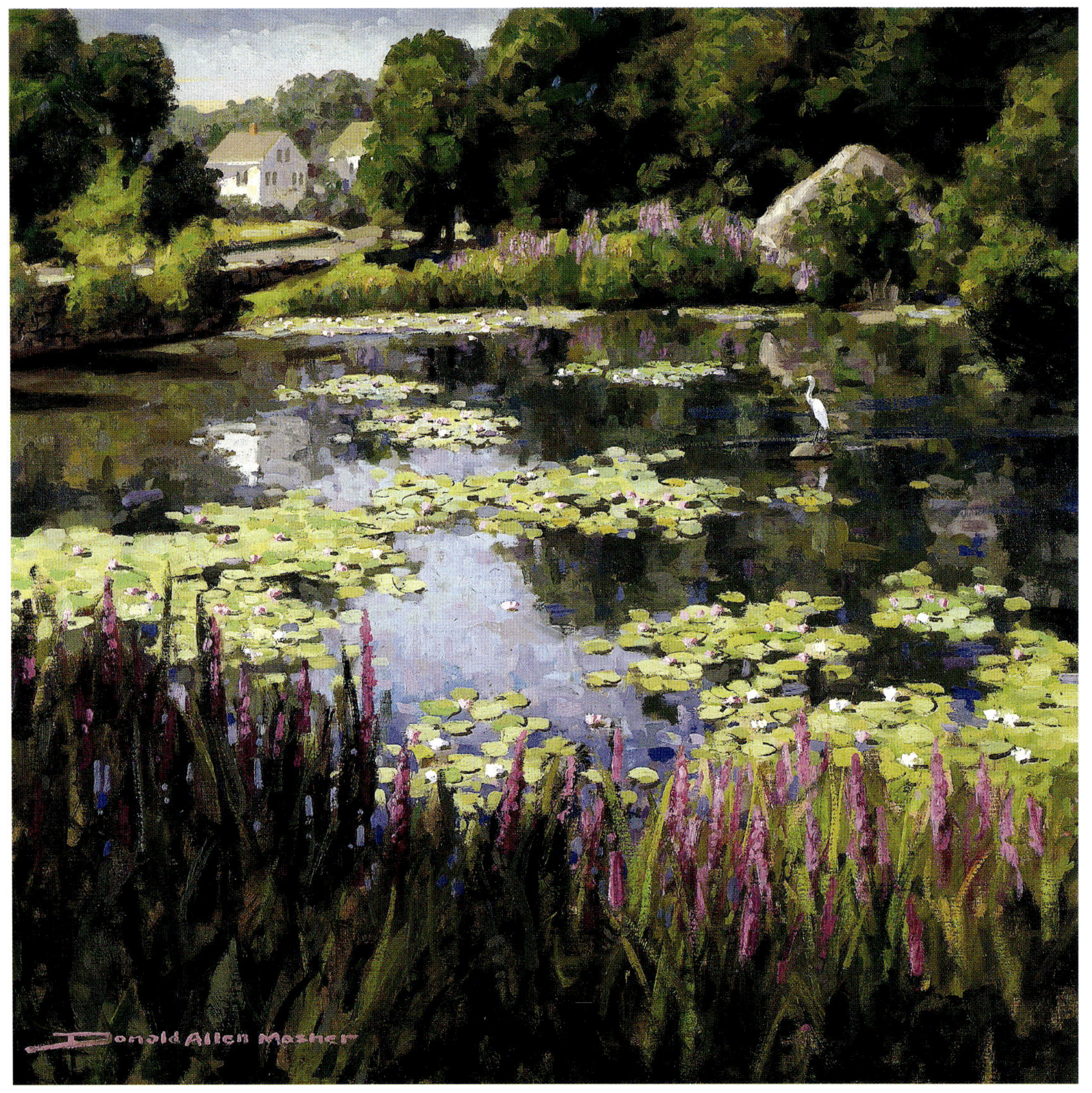

Beside Still Waters (30 x 30)

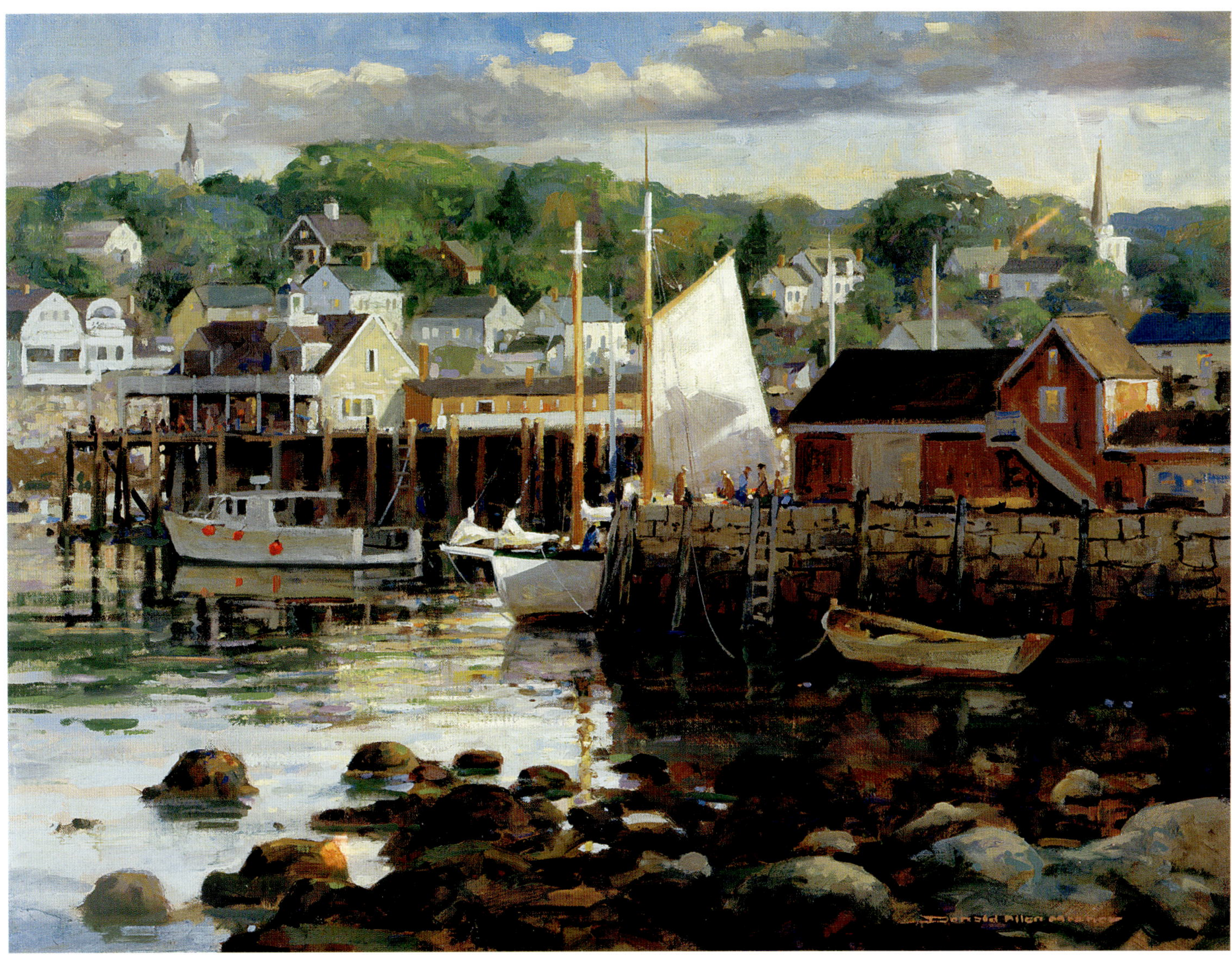

Rockport Inner Harbor (25 x 30)

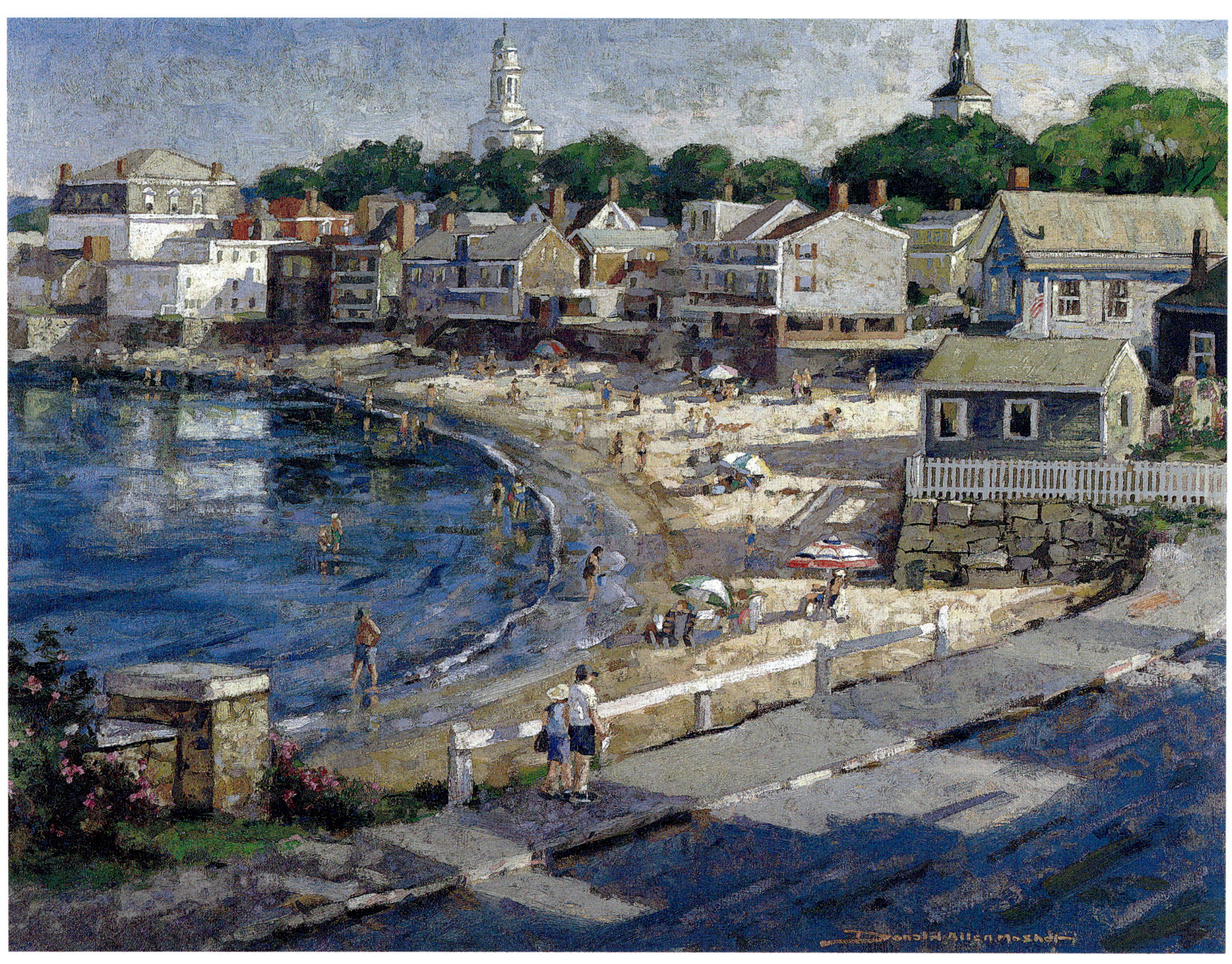

Front Beach, Rockport (25 x 30)

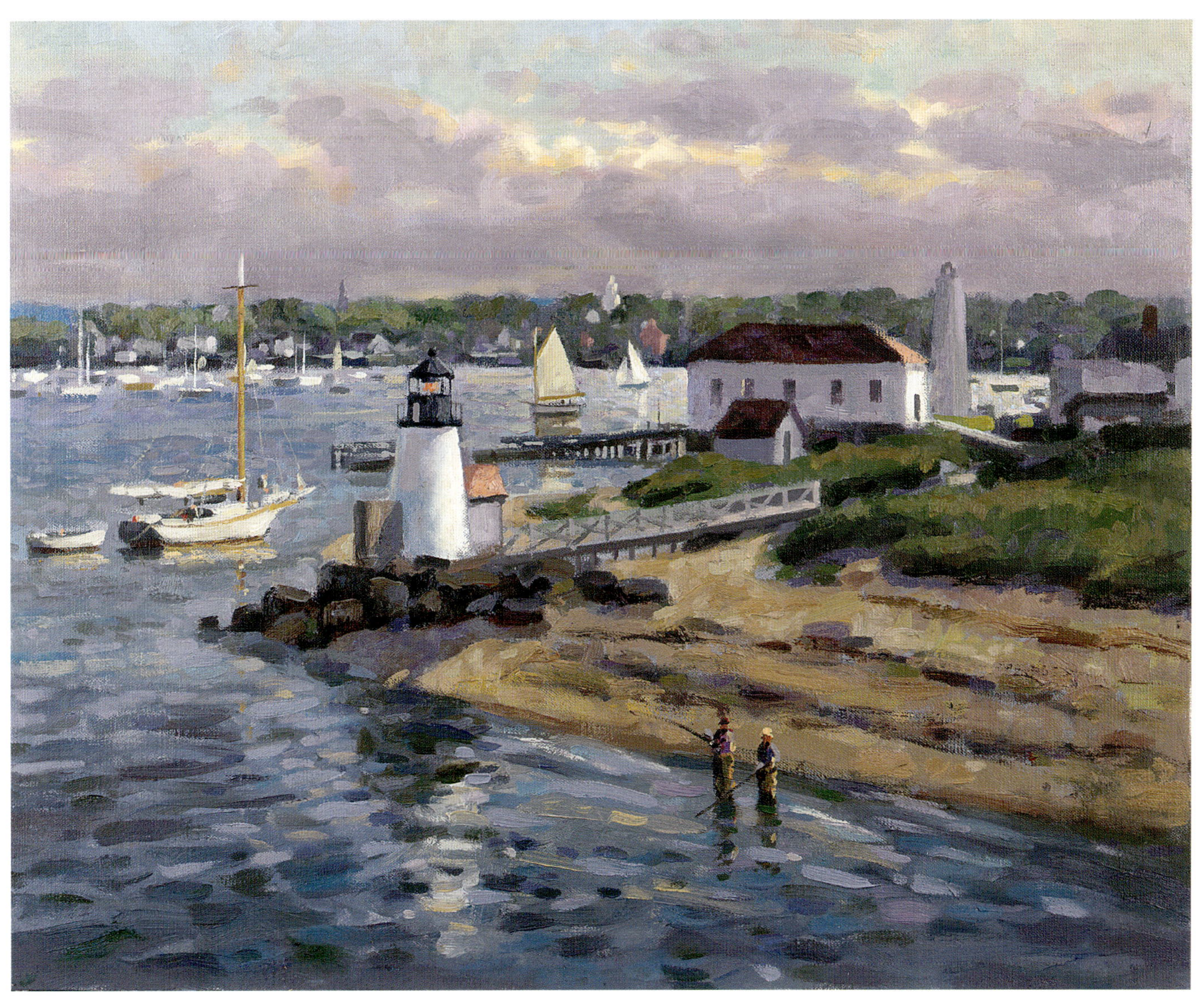

Late Day, Nantucket (20 x 24)

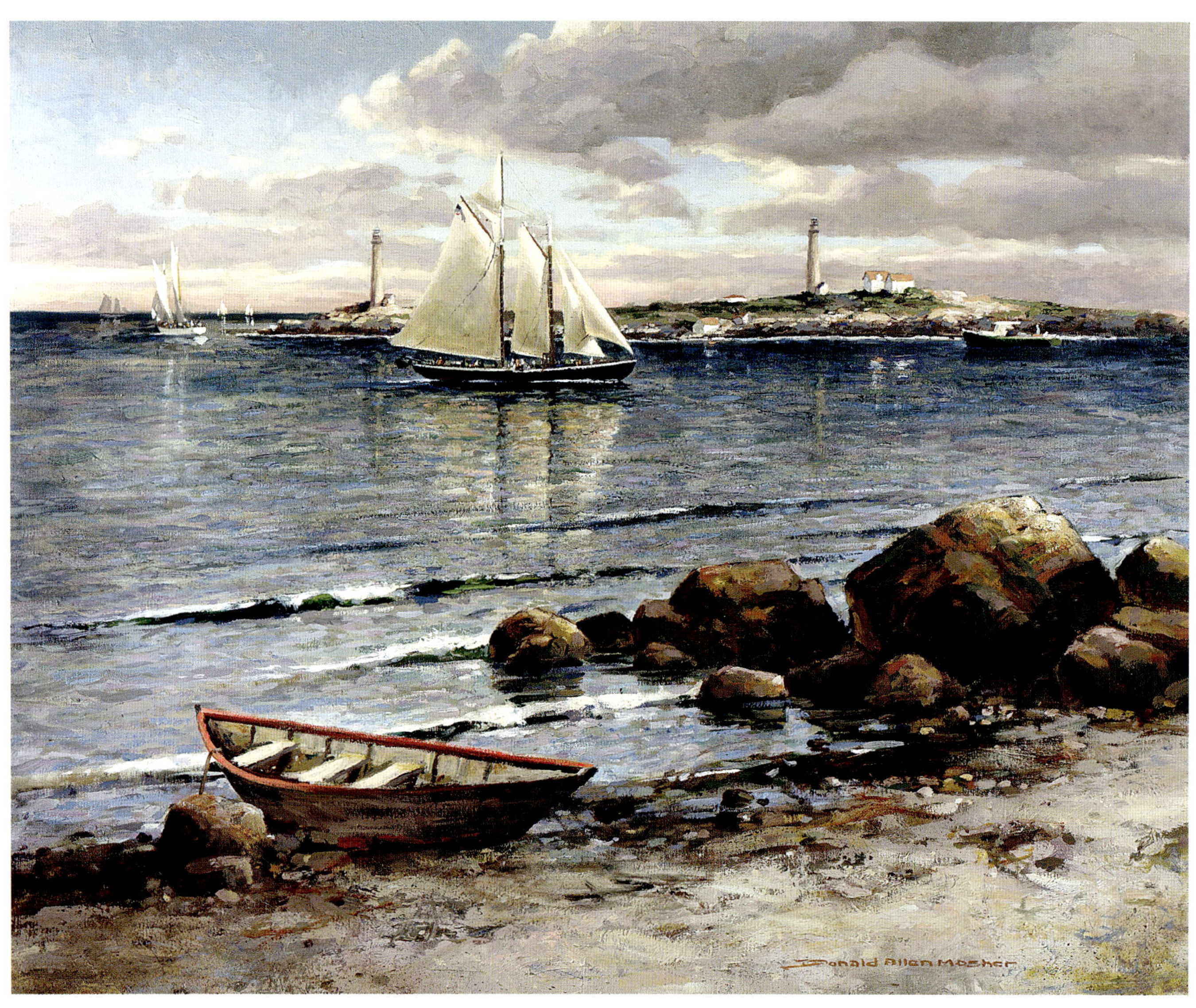

Adventure, Near Thacher Island (30 x 36)

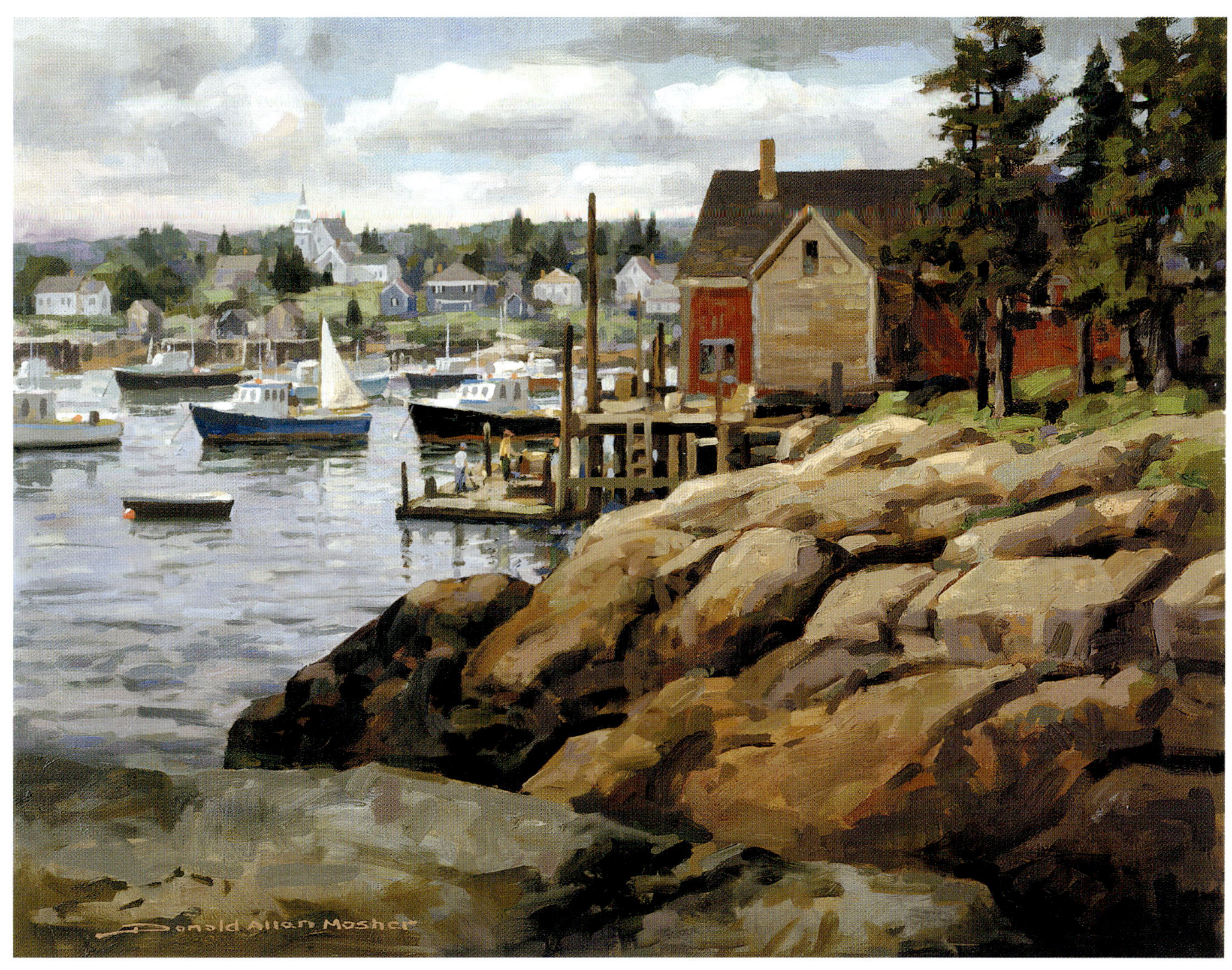

Lobstering, Corea, Maine (20 x 28)

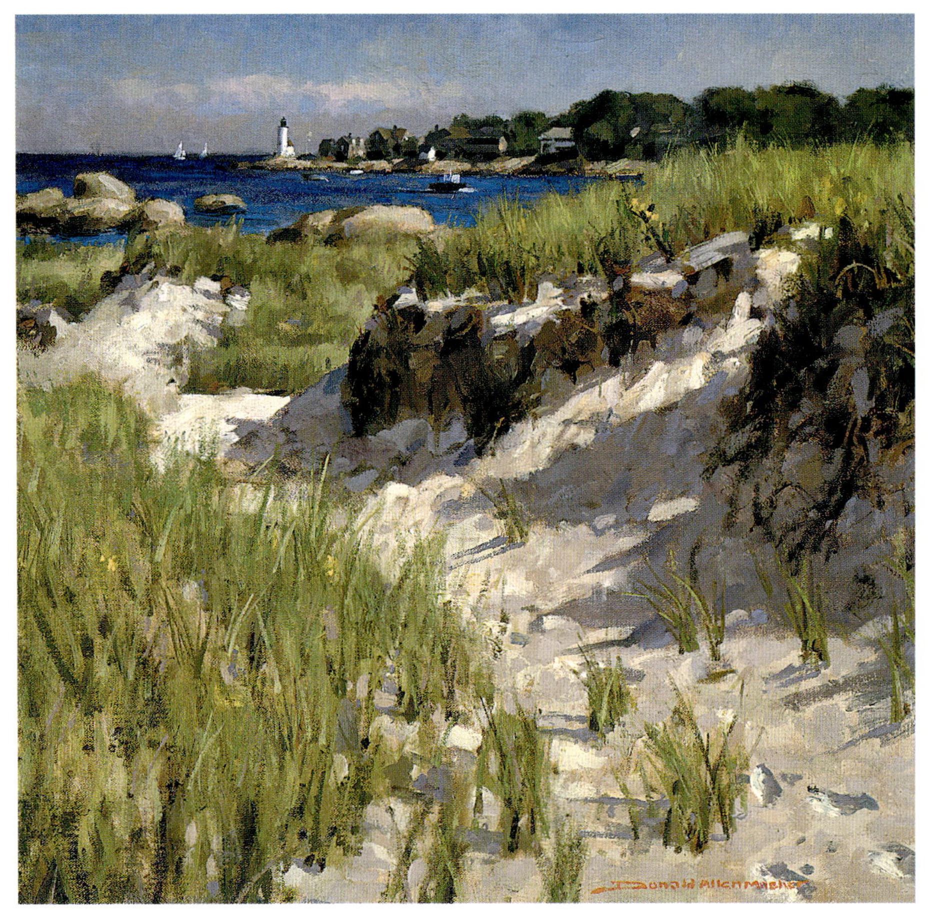

September Dunes, Wingaersheek (24 x 24)

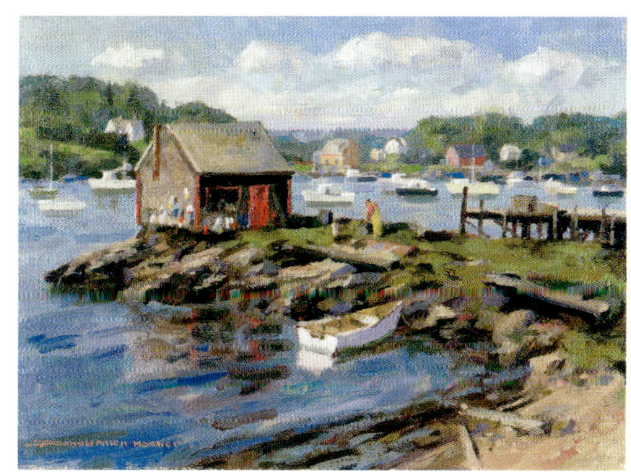

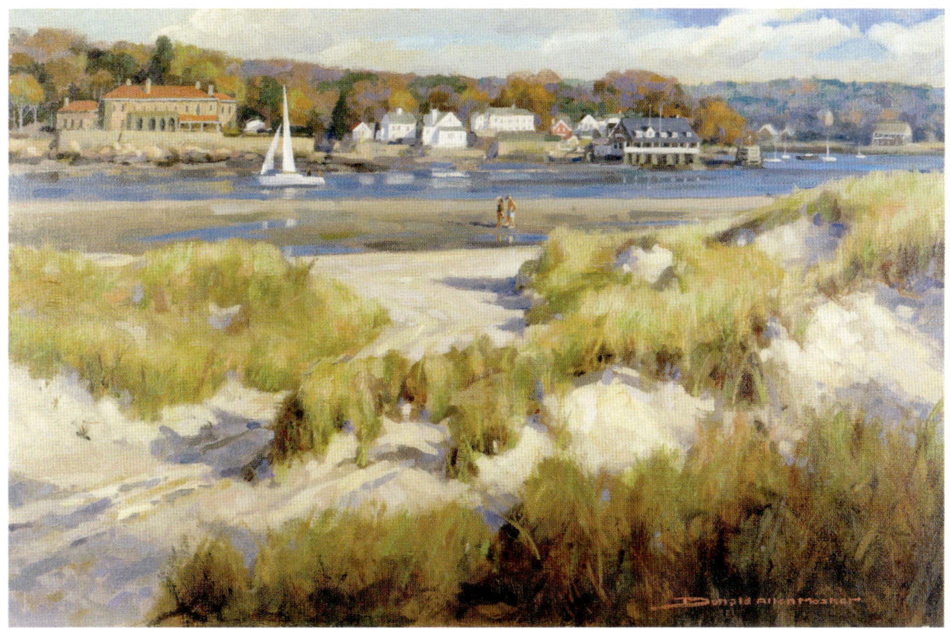

Top: Bailey Island, Maine (12 x 16)
Bottom: Across the Annisquam (20 x 30)

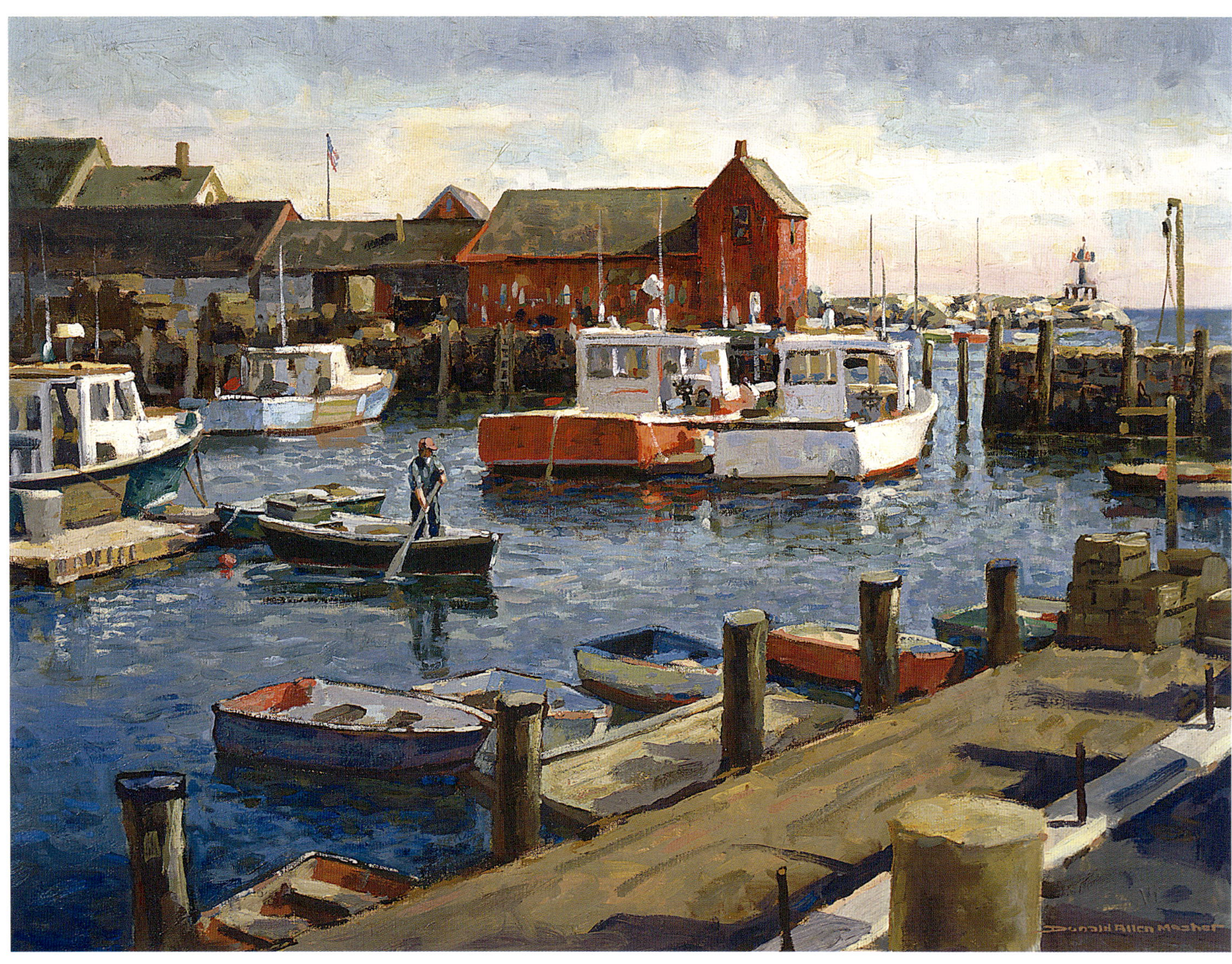

End of the Day (24 x 30)

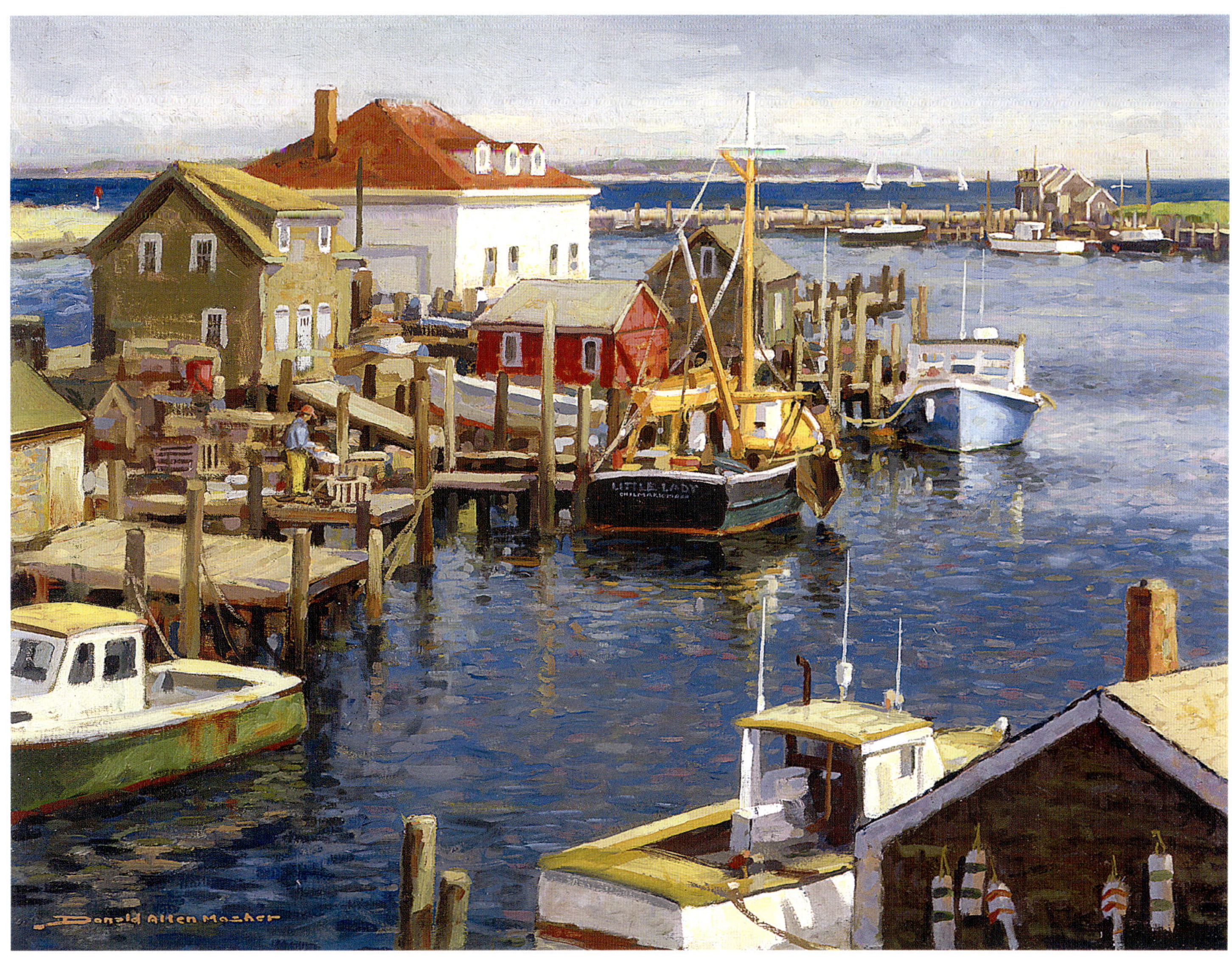

A Working Harbor (24 x 30)

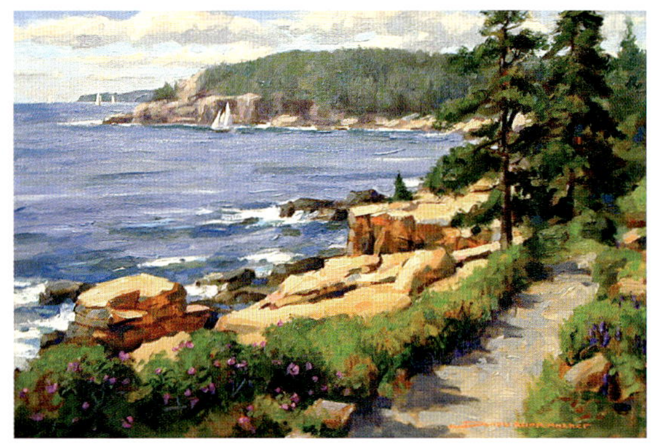

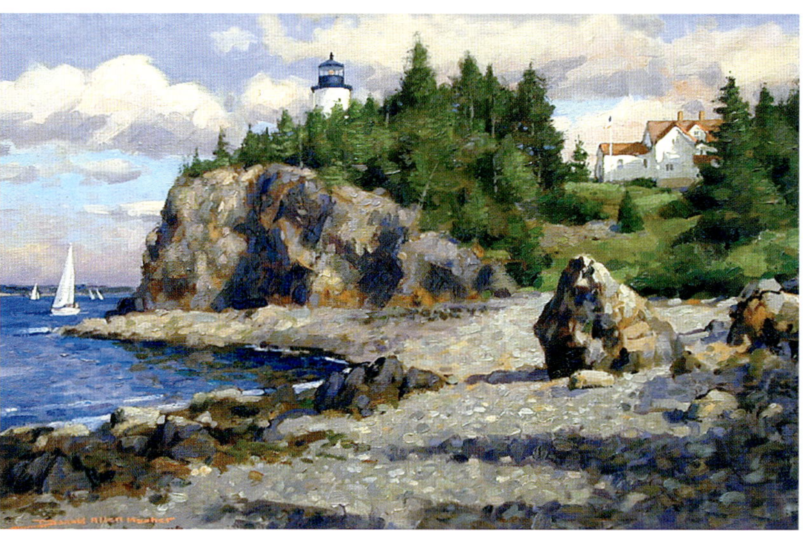

Top left: Shore Path, Acadia (14 x 22)
Top right: Owl's Head Light (20 x 30)

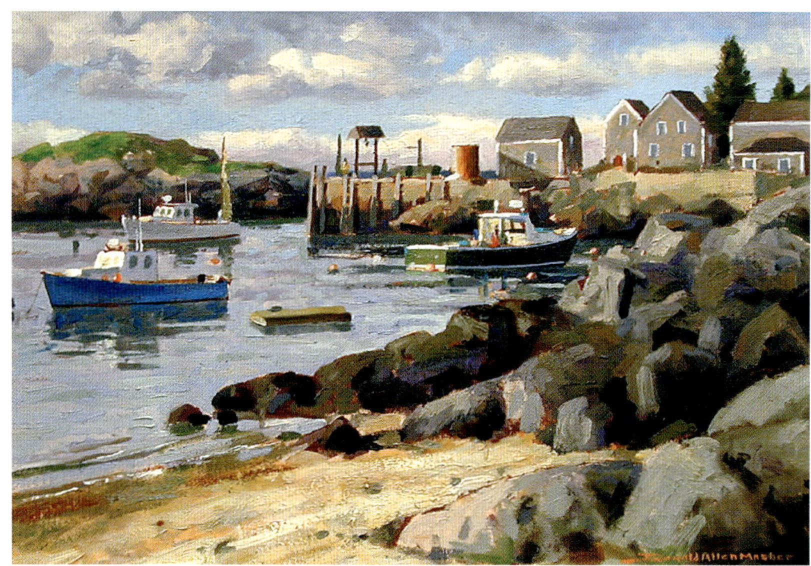

Bottom: Fish Beach, Monhegan (14 x 18)

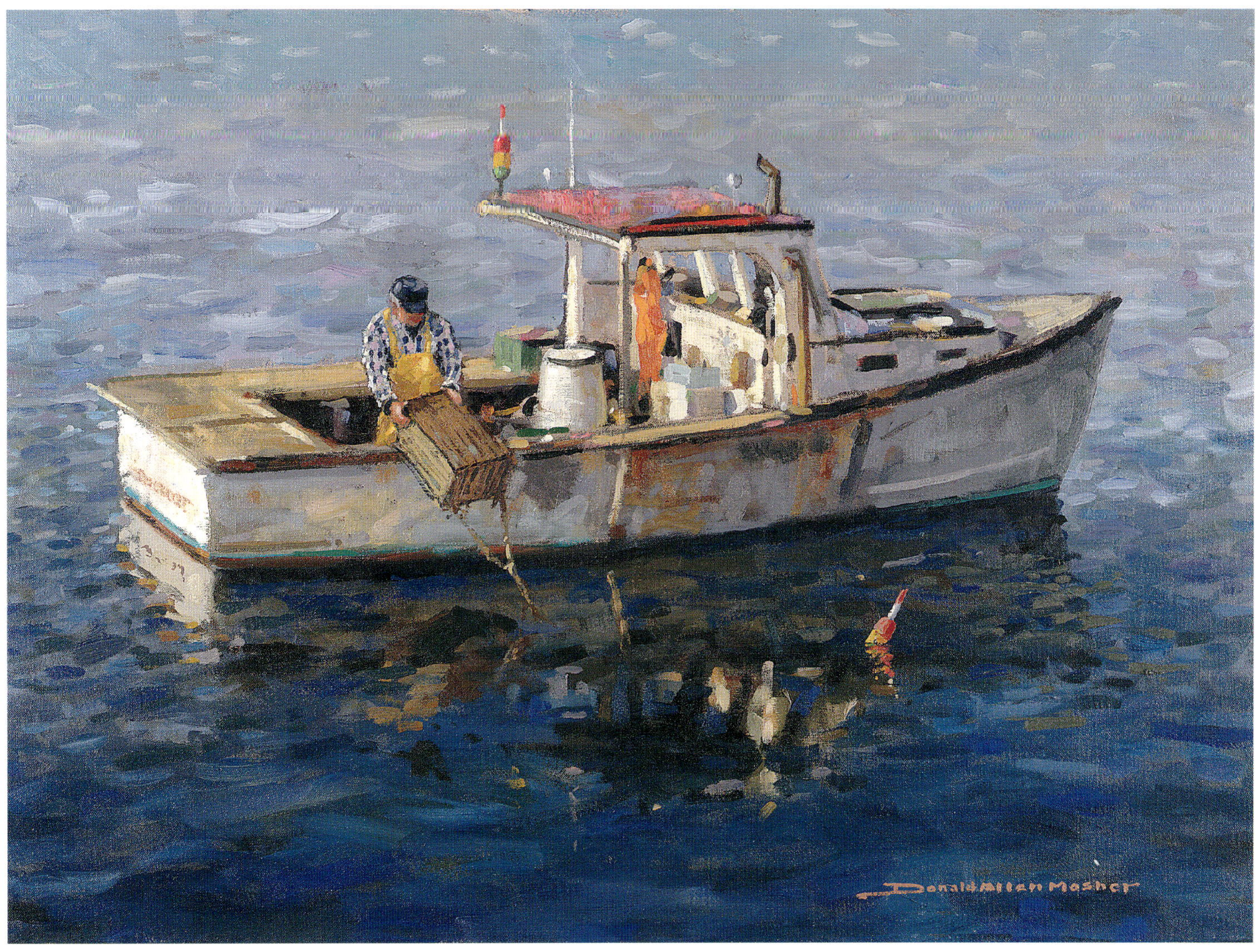

Hauling Traps (26 x 36)

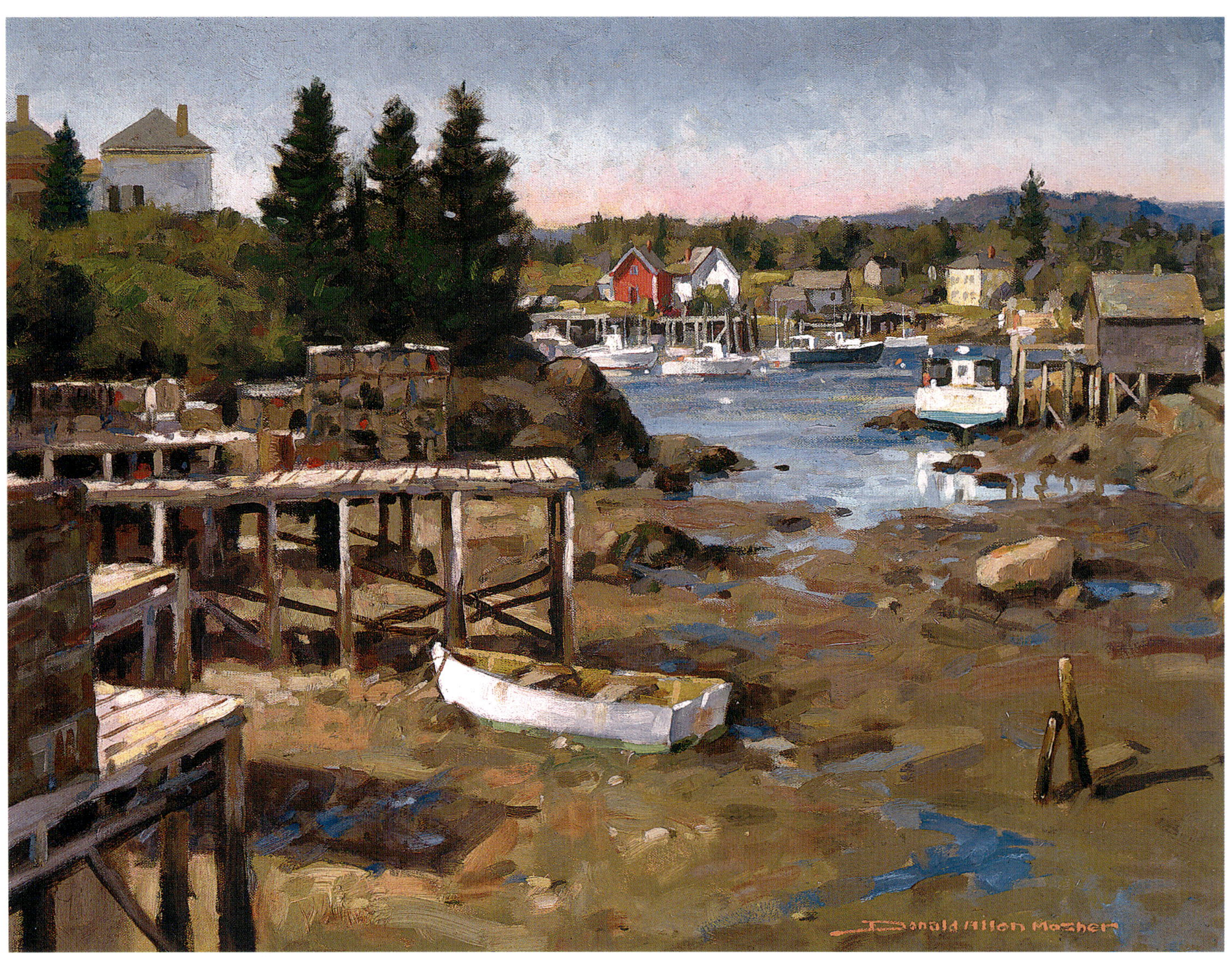

Low Tide, Corea (24 x 30)

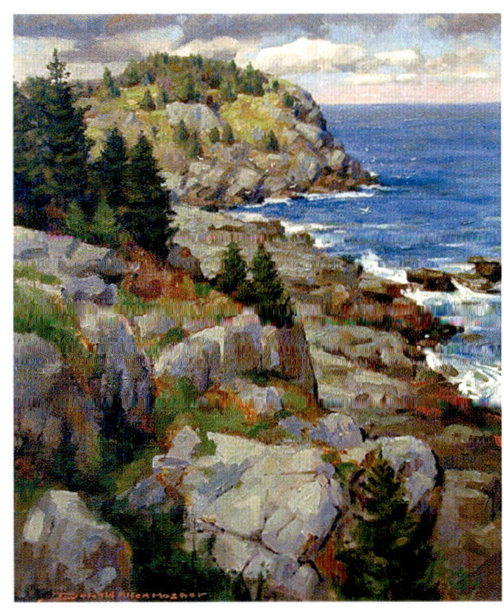

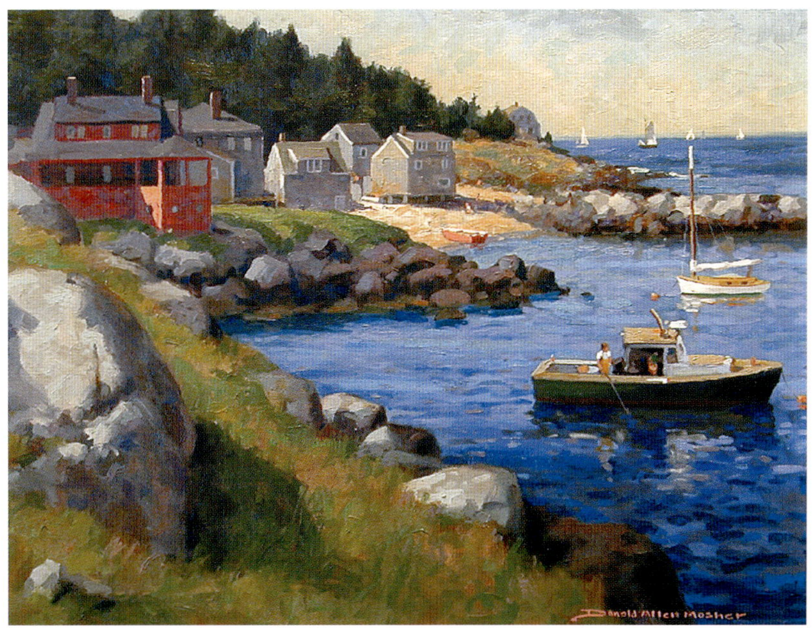

Top: White Head Cliff (30 x 24)
Right: May Day, Monhegan Island (16 x 20)

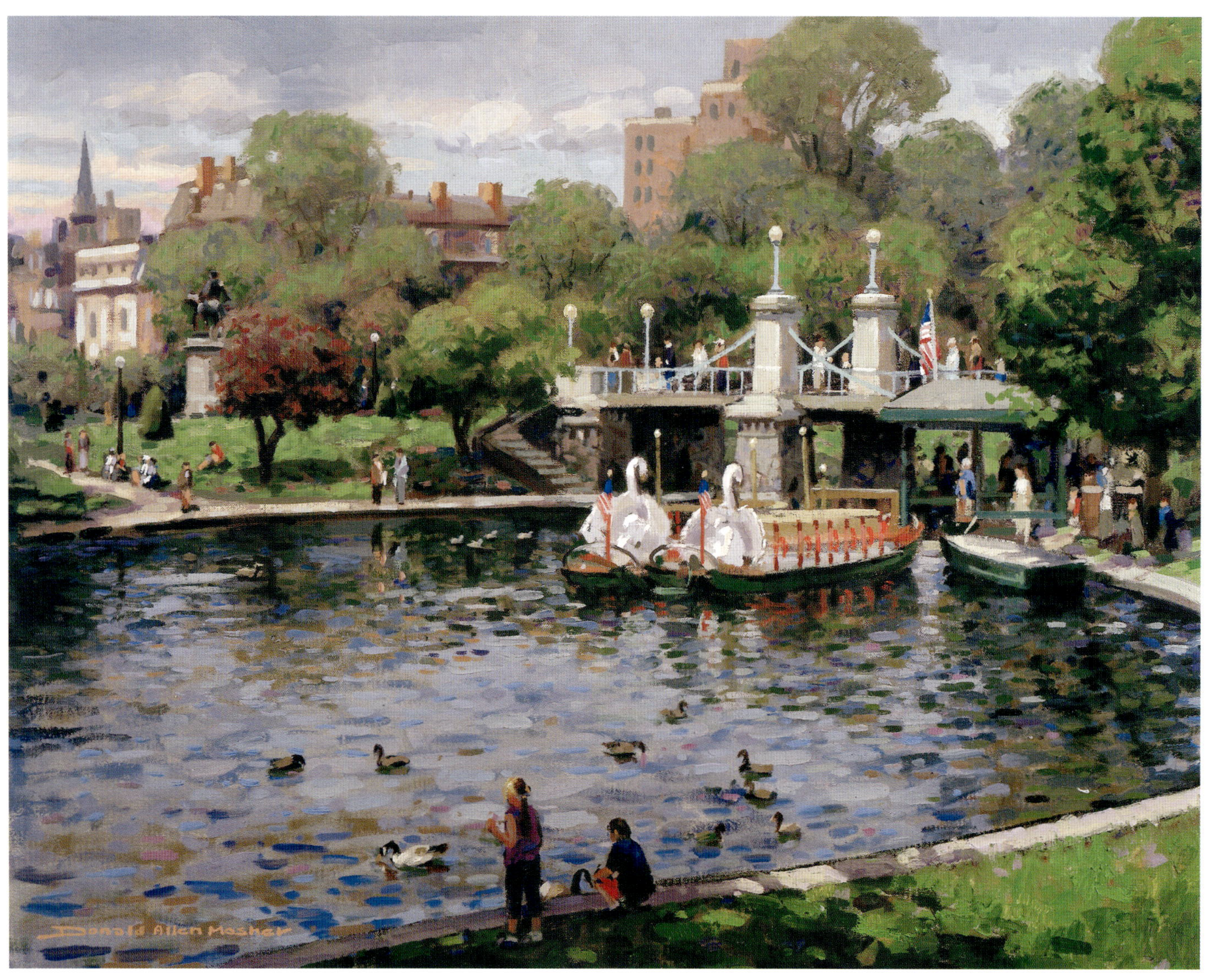

Make Way for Boston (26 x 32)

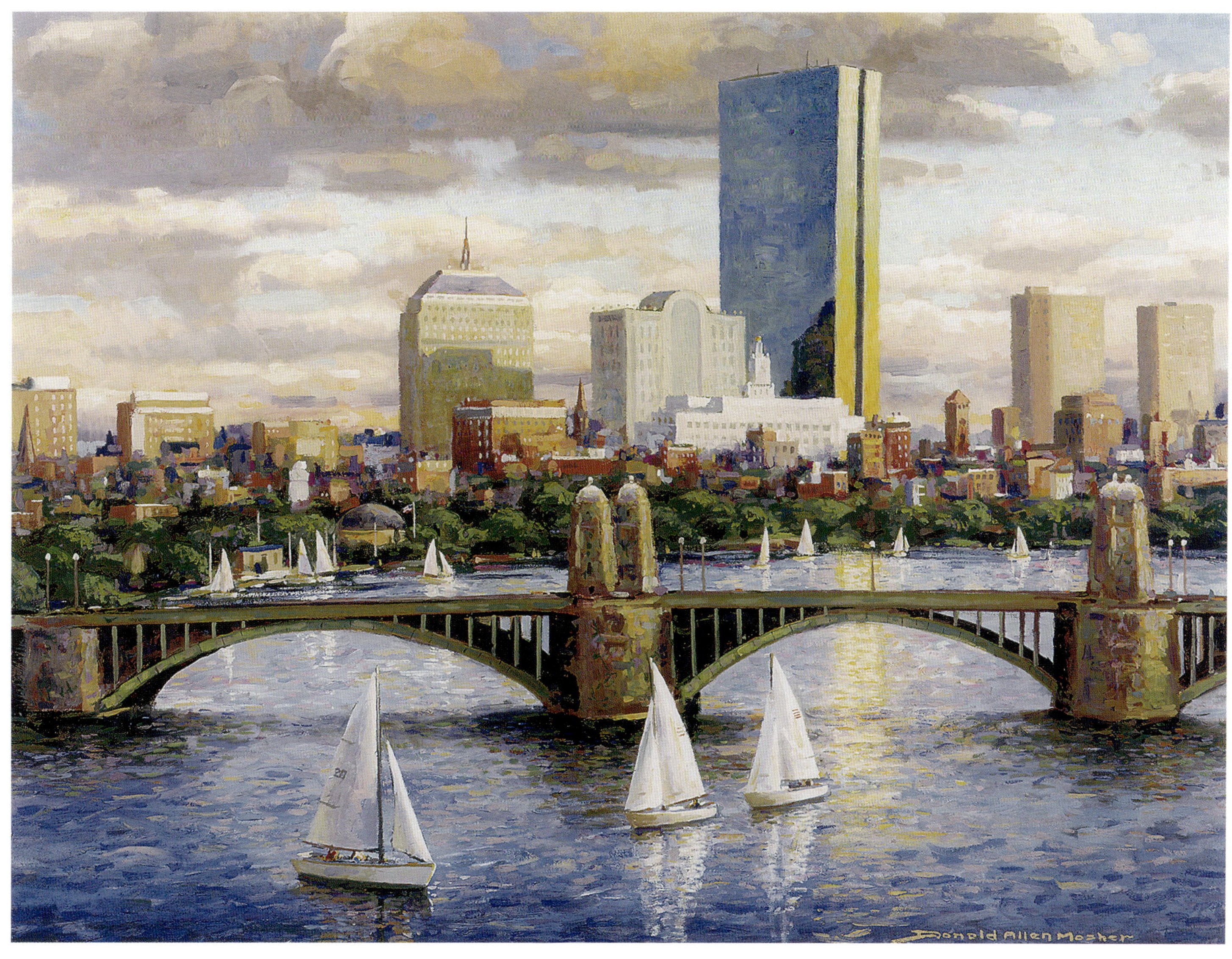

Sailing the Charles (30 x 36)

AUTUMN

The landscape painter must walk in the fields with a humble mind. No arrogant man was ever permitted to see nature in all her beauty.
—John Constable

Autumn sends me to Vermont and New Hampshire. I usually make a couple of trips right after Columbus Day. Nothing beats the sound of a waterfall or a river rushing beneath a covered bridge. I don't think there's any sight more beautiful than bright fall colors of red, yellow, orange, and green with a snow-covered background like Mt. Mansfield or Mt. Washington.

Trying to capture the brilliance of a fall landscape is nearly impossible. Every painter is inferior in front of a mountain-side in full foliage. You can't take the paint straight out of the tube and make it as brilliant as you see it. When I compare the colors in my painting with the actual colors of a fall scene, the painting seems to fall far short. Only at home in my studio can I make the colors harmonize to give me a sense of where I've been.

I also like to paint late in the fall when the trees have shed most of their leaves and have turned a more rustic red and ochre. Falling leaves reveal the structure of the trees. There's a crispness in the air, and you know that soon there will be snow.

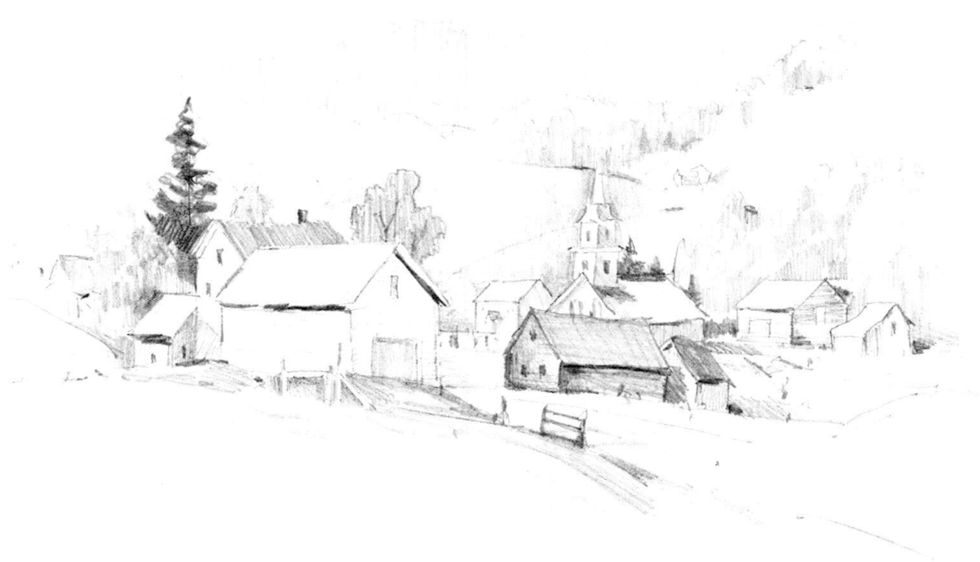

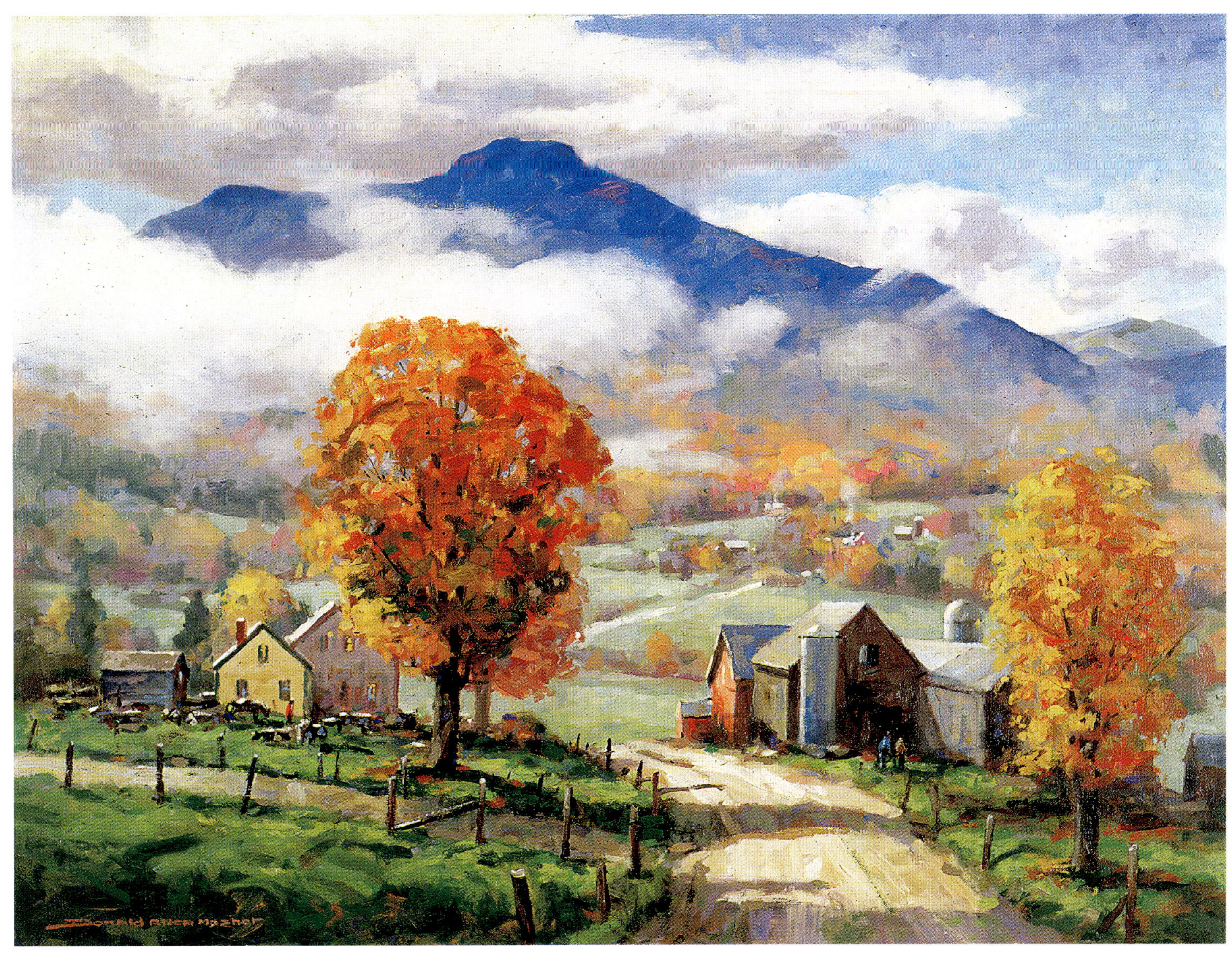

Upper Valley Road (30 x 36)

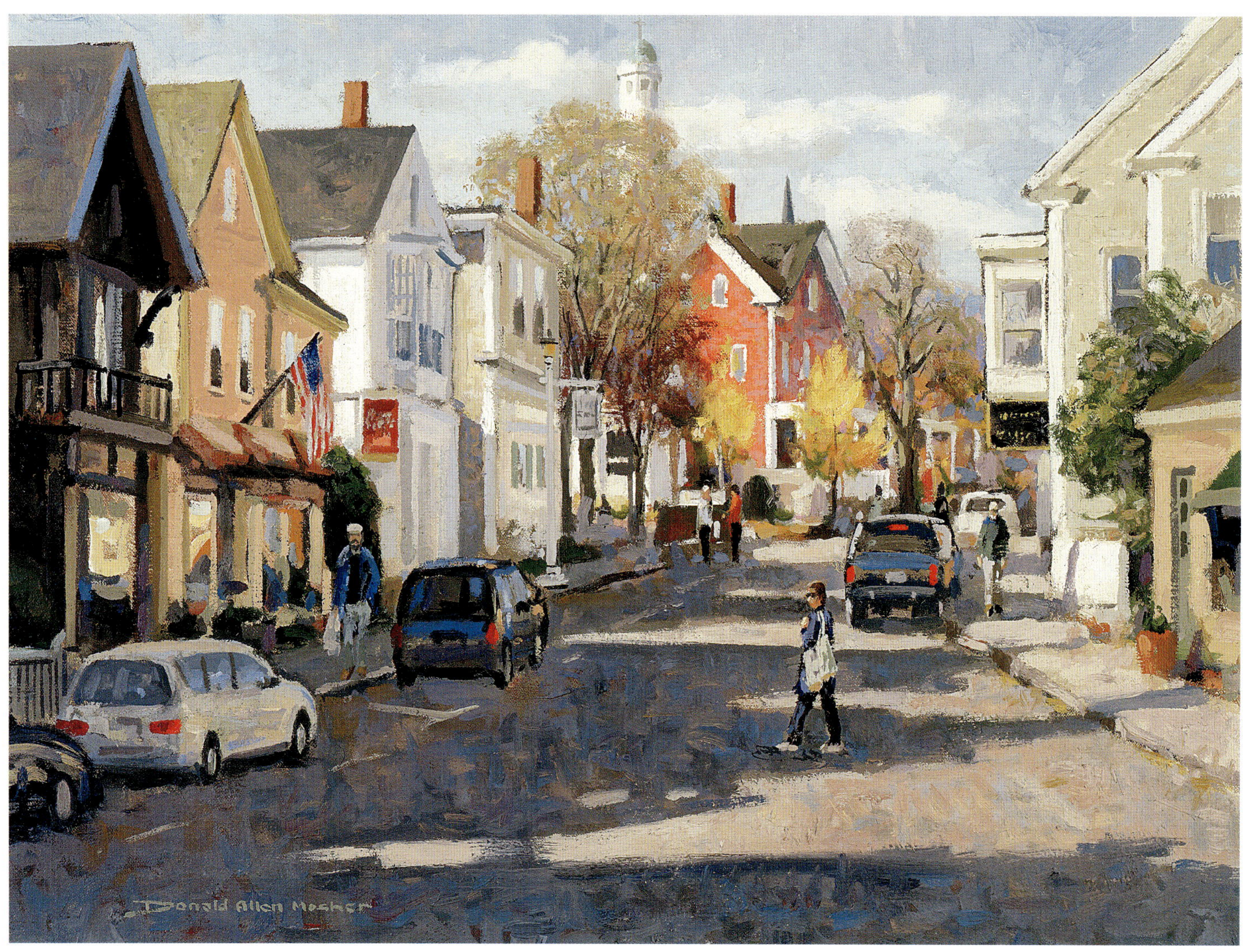

Main Street, Rockport (24 x 32)

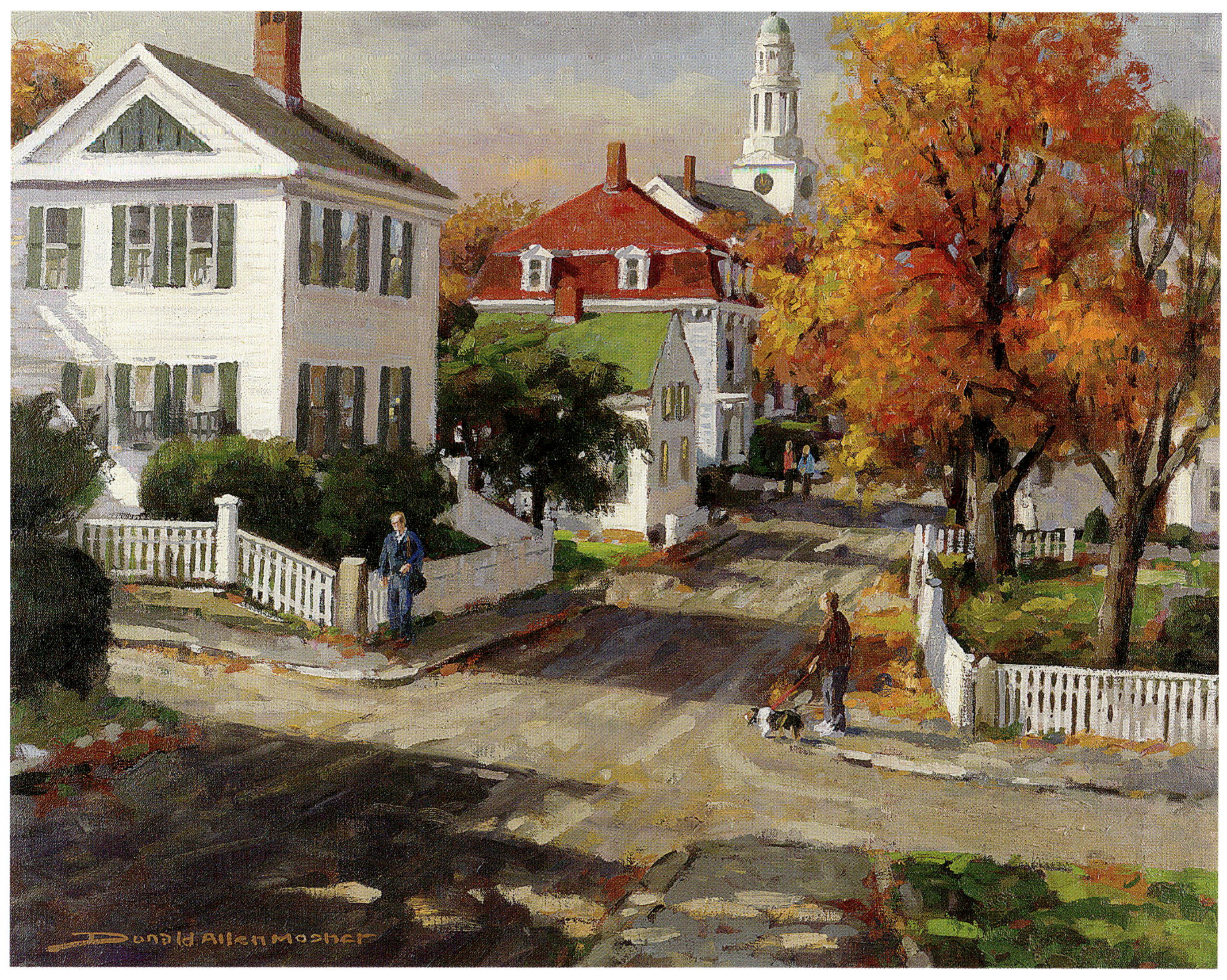

The Crossroads, Rockport (25 x 30)

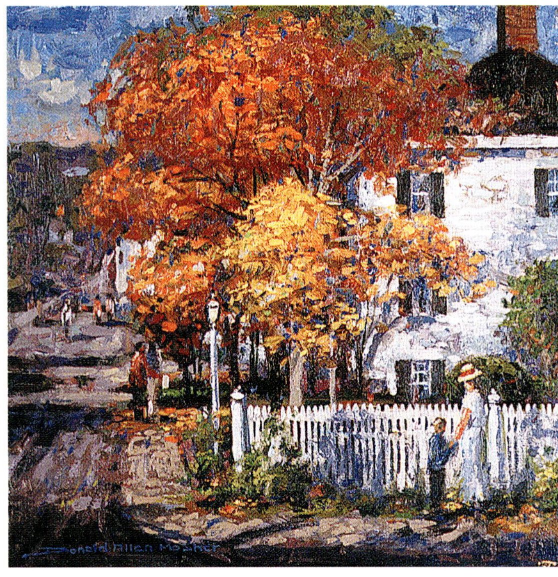

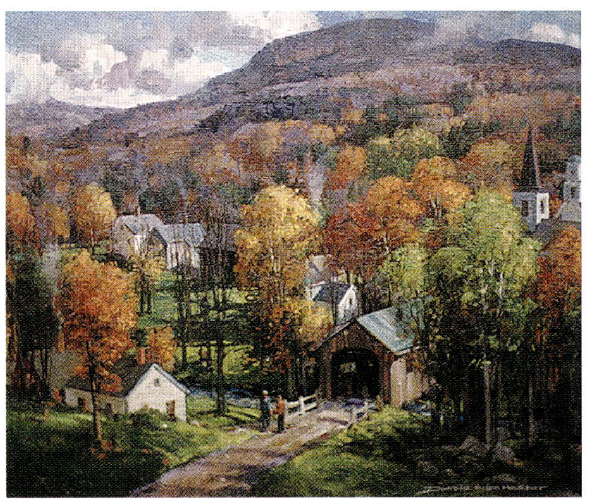

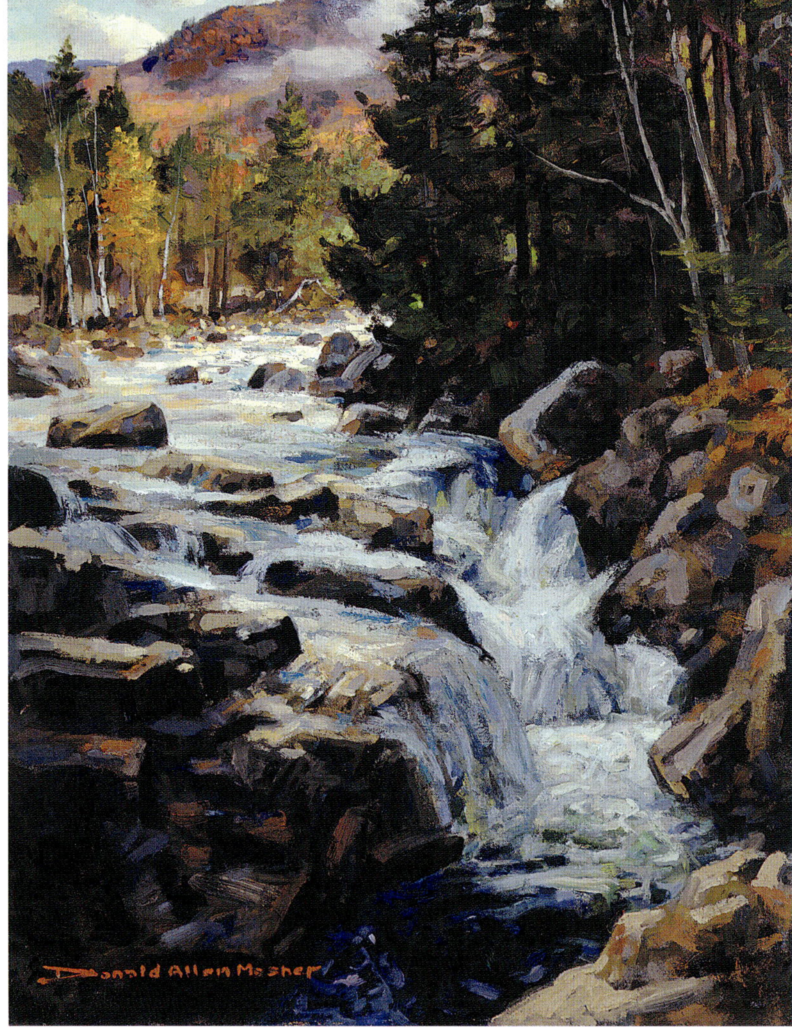

Top left: Autumn Stroll (16 x 16)
Bottom Left: Over Waterville, Vermont (20 x 24)
Right: Upper Falls, Kancamagus (30 x 24)

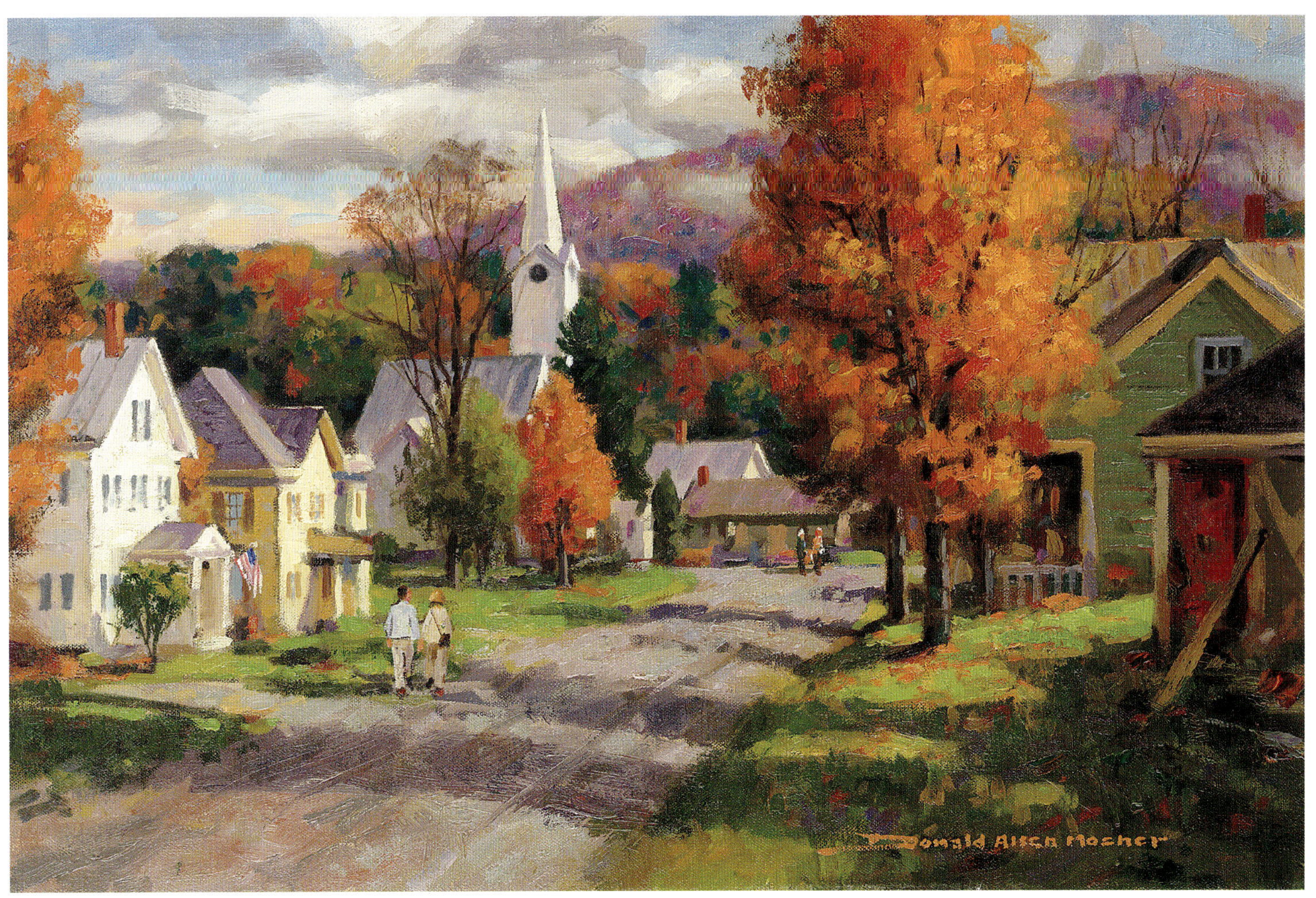

Sunday Morning (16 x 24)

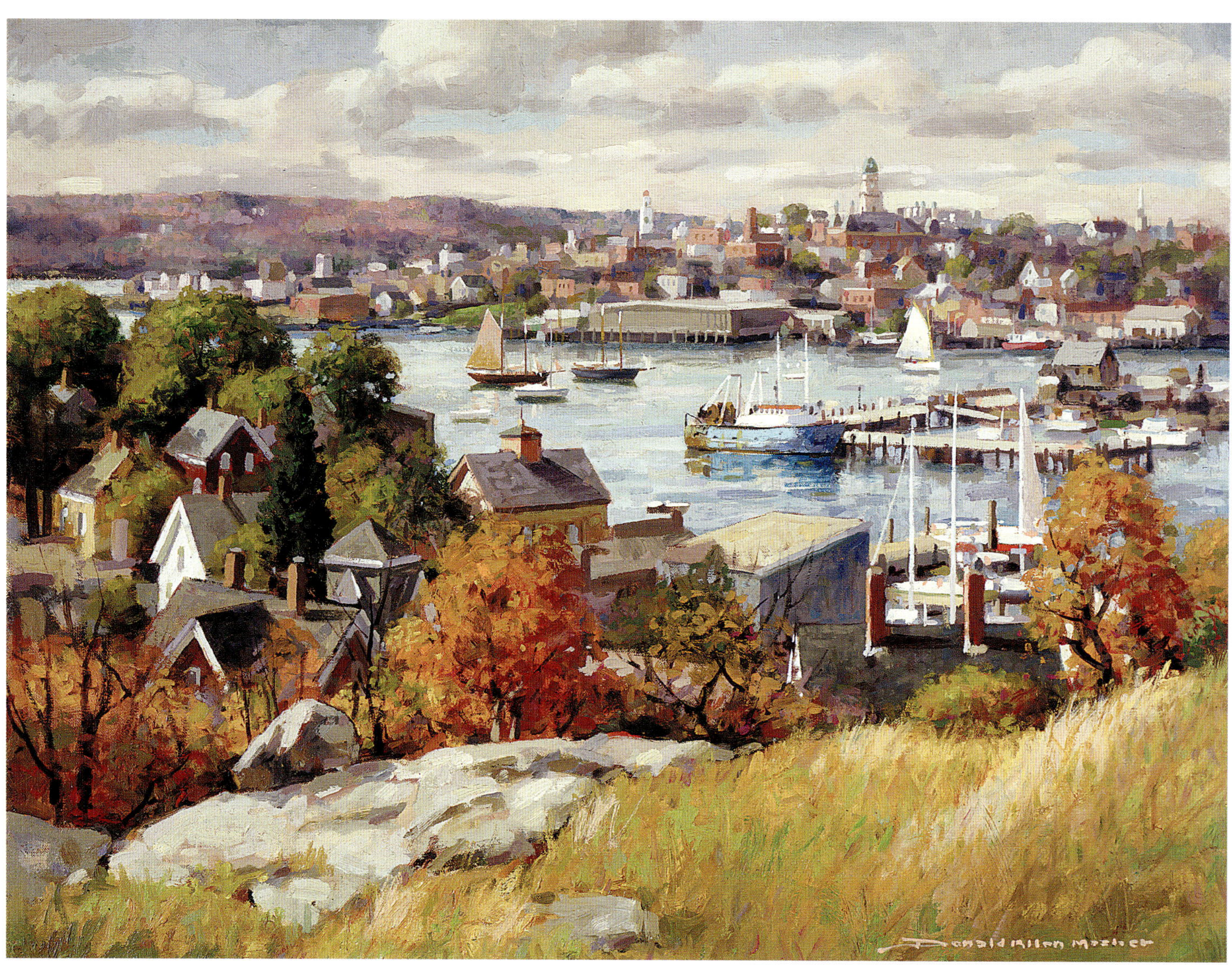

Changing Colors, Gloucester (26 x 32)

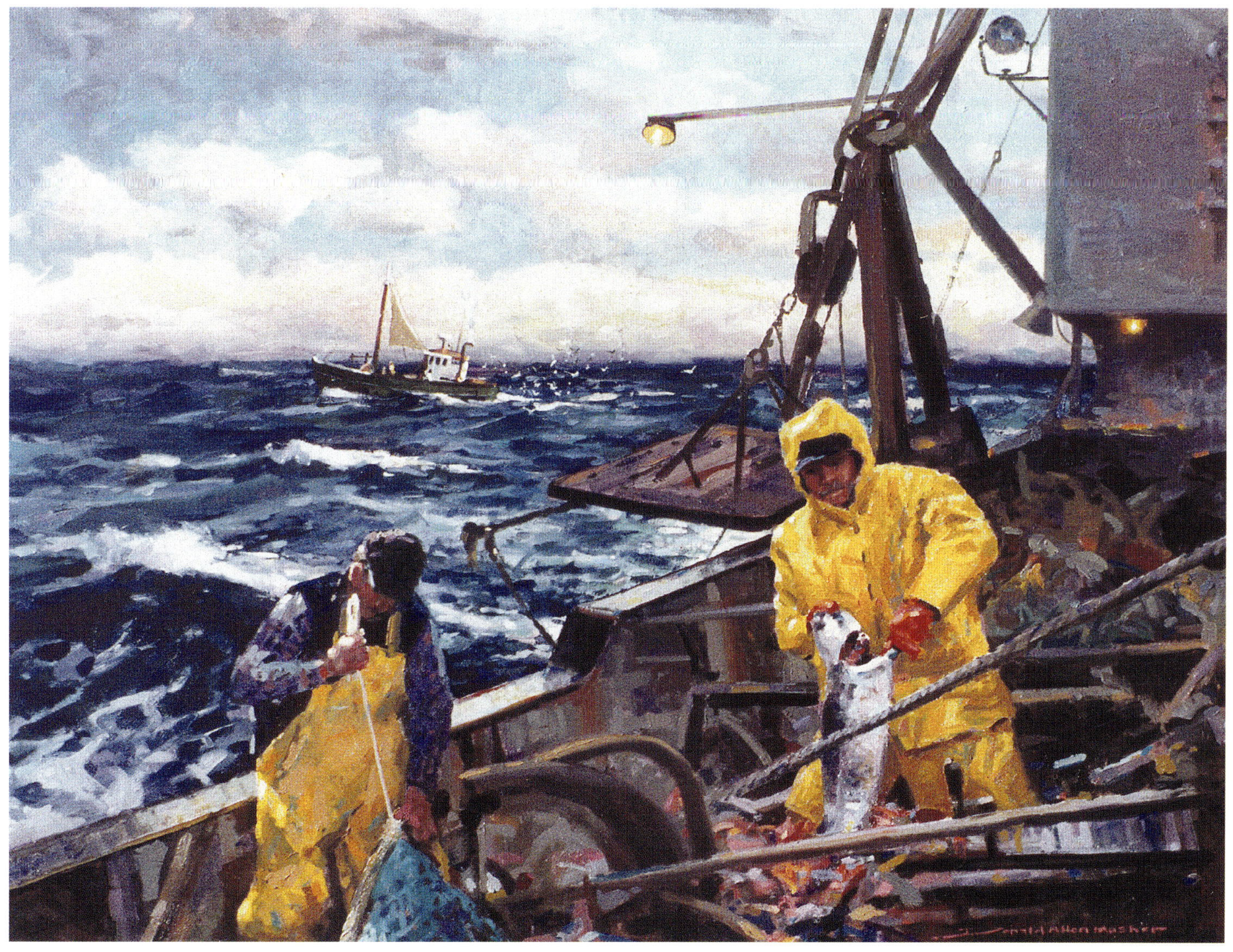

The Gloucestermen (40 x 50)

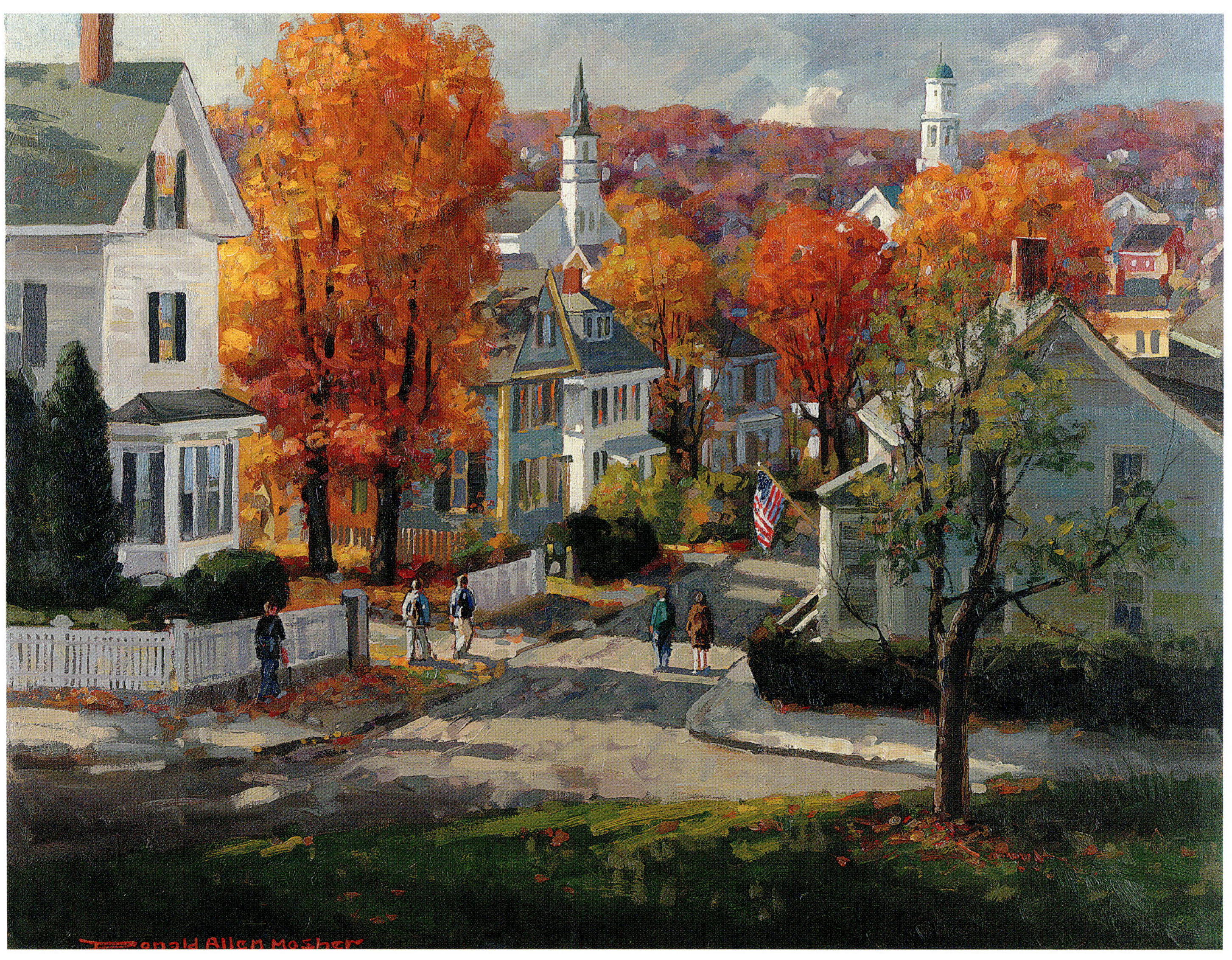

School's Out (26 x 32)

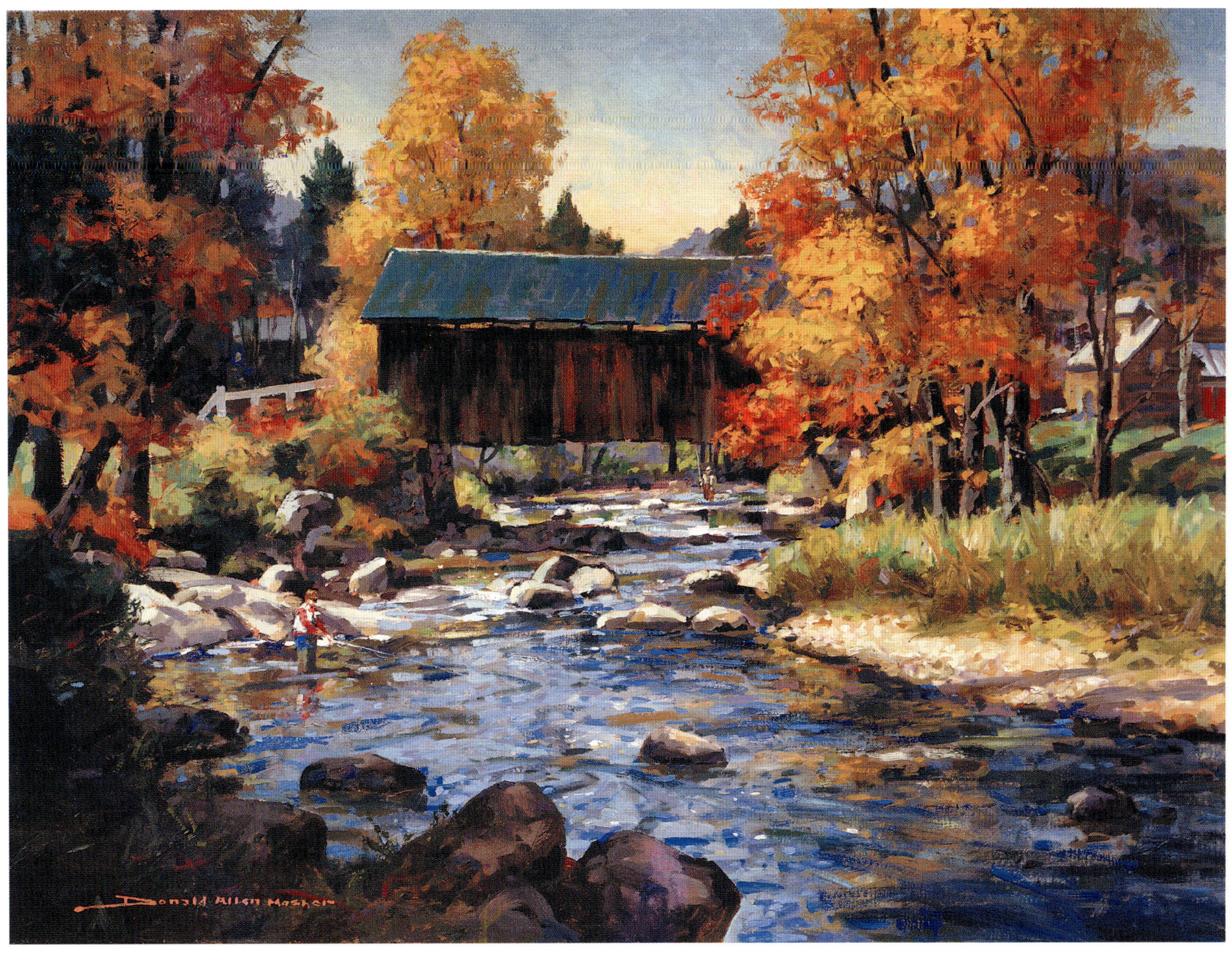

Fishing the Lamoile River (30 x 40)

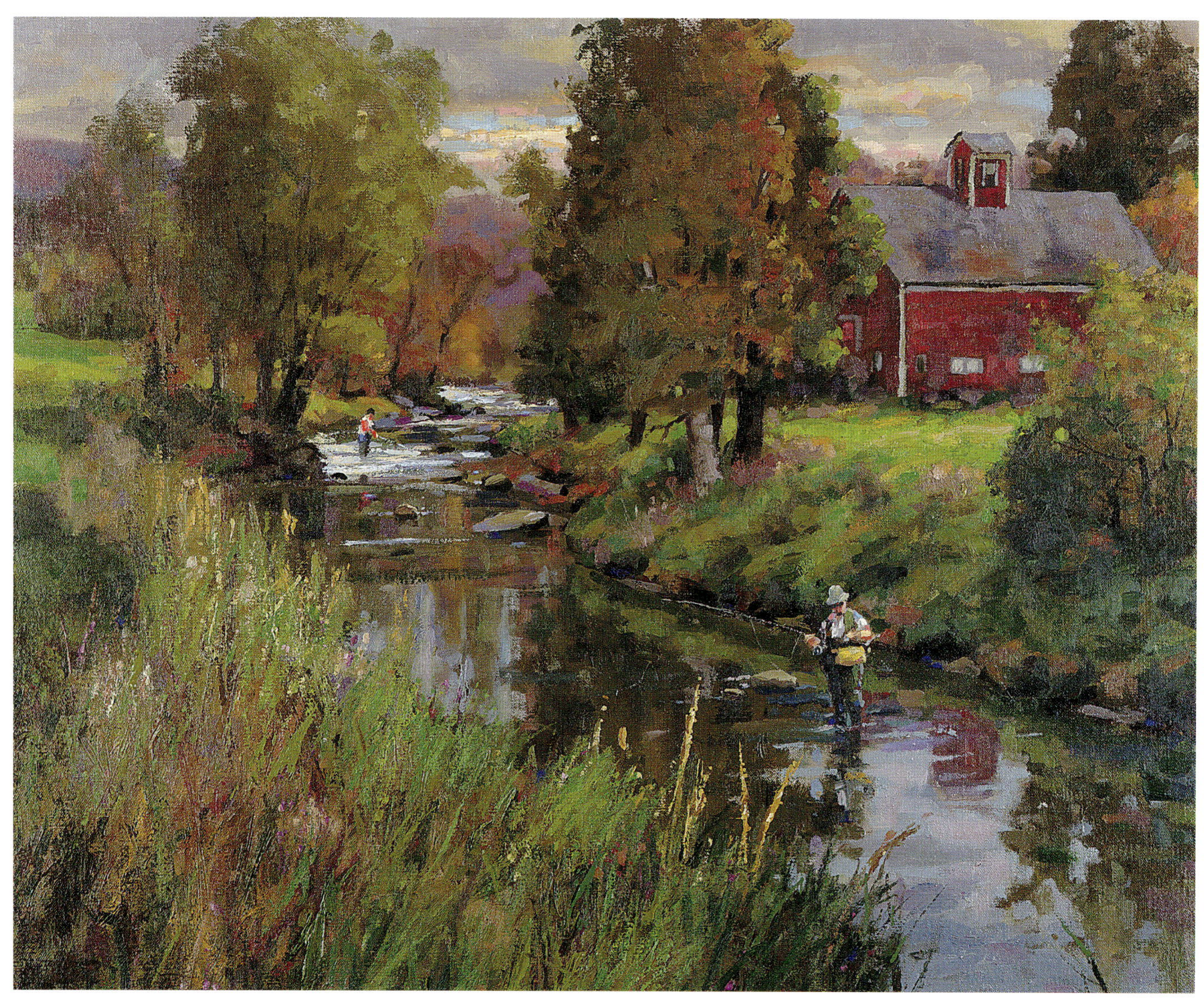

Fly Fishing (26 x 32)

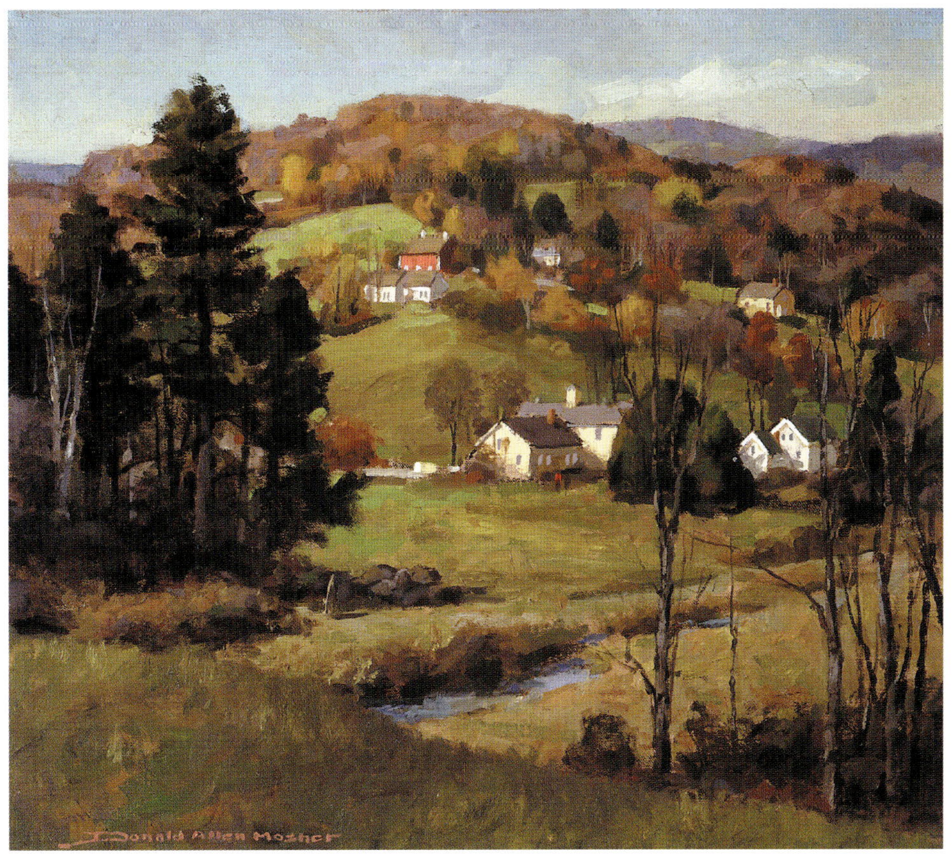

When we walk, we naturally go to the fields and the woods; what would become of us if we walked only in a garden or a mall?

—Henry David Thoreau

Woodstock Horse Farm (24 x 24)

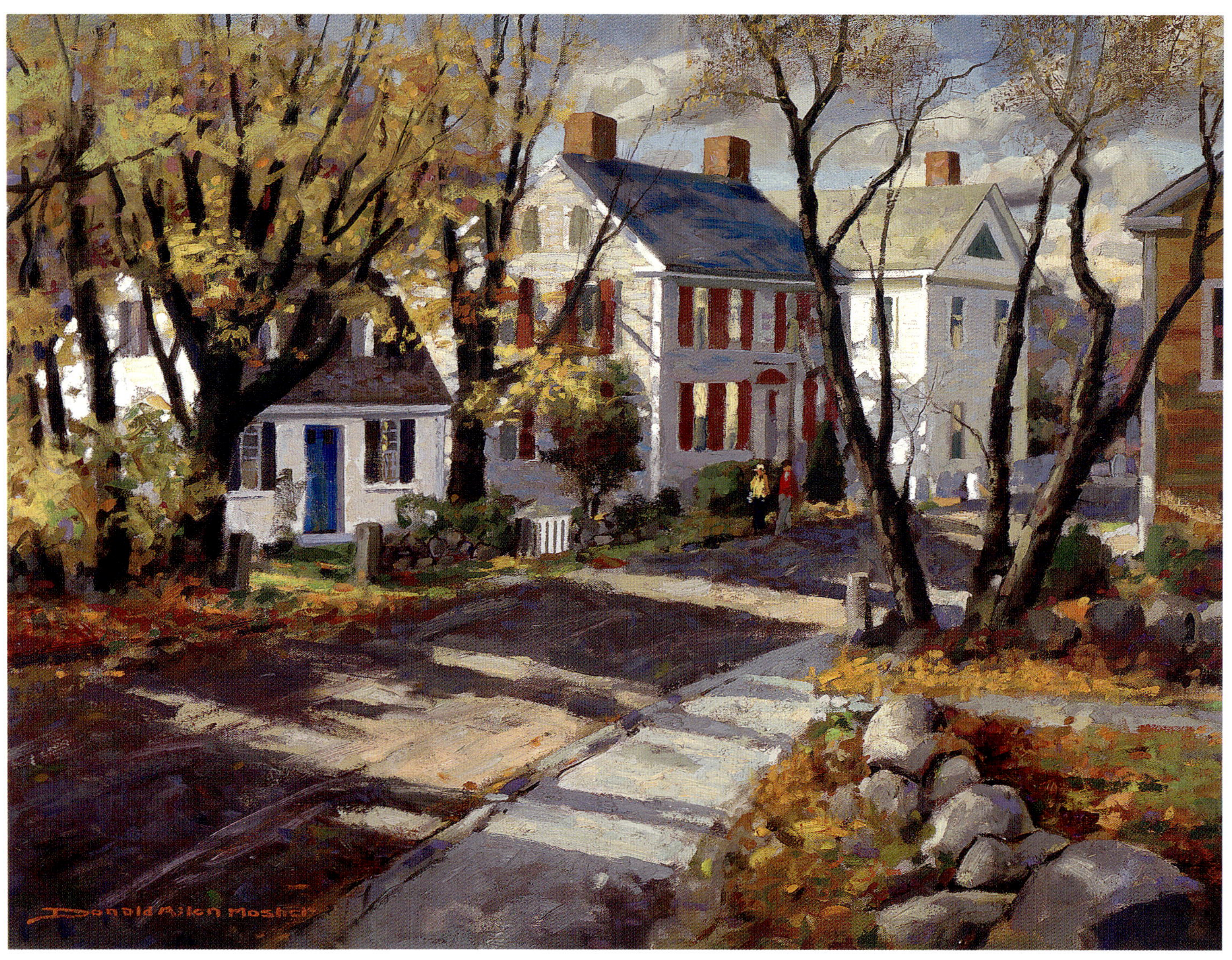

Late Day, Rockport (26 x 34)

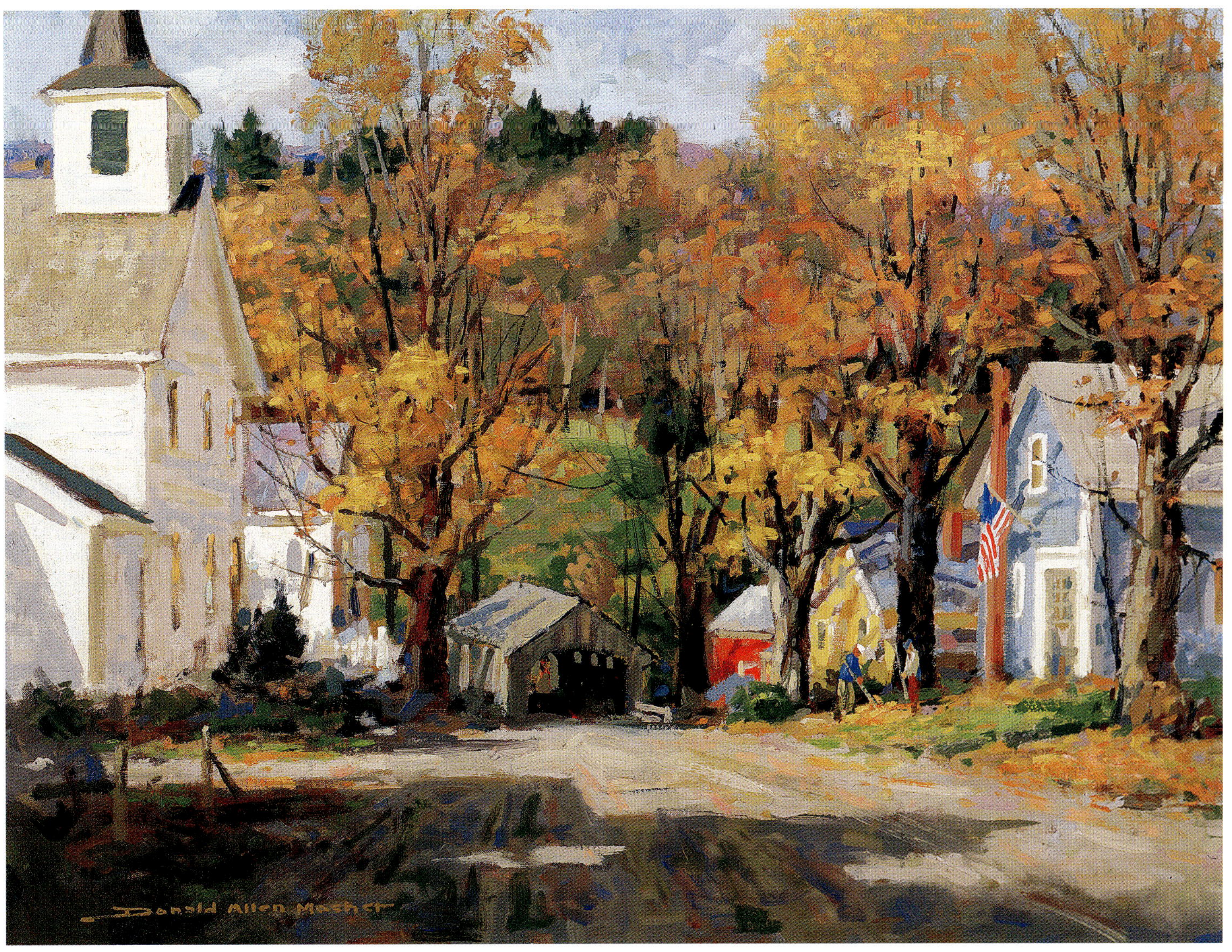

Autumn's Passage, Vermont (25 x 30)

WINTER

A work of art is the social act of a solitary man.
—William Butler Yeats

If I am best known for my snow scenes, it is probably because I love to paint them. I love the silence of the snow, and being alone with it. I can't think of anything more fun than standing knee-deep in a drift and trying to capture the colors and the essence of snow. I love the fact that snow is not really white. It contains every color. I look for the warmth in snow from a reflected building, the yellows where the sun hits it, the blues in a deep shadow.

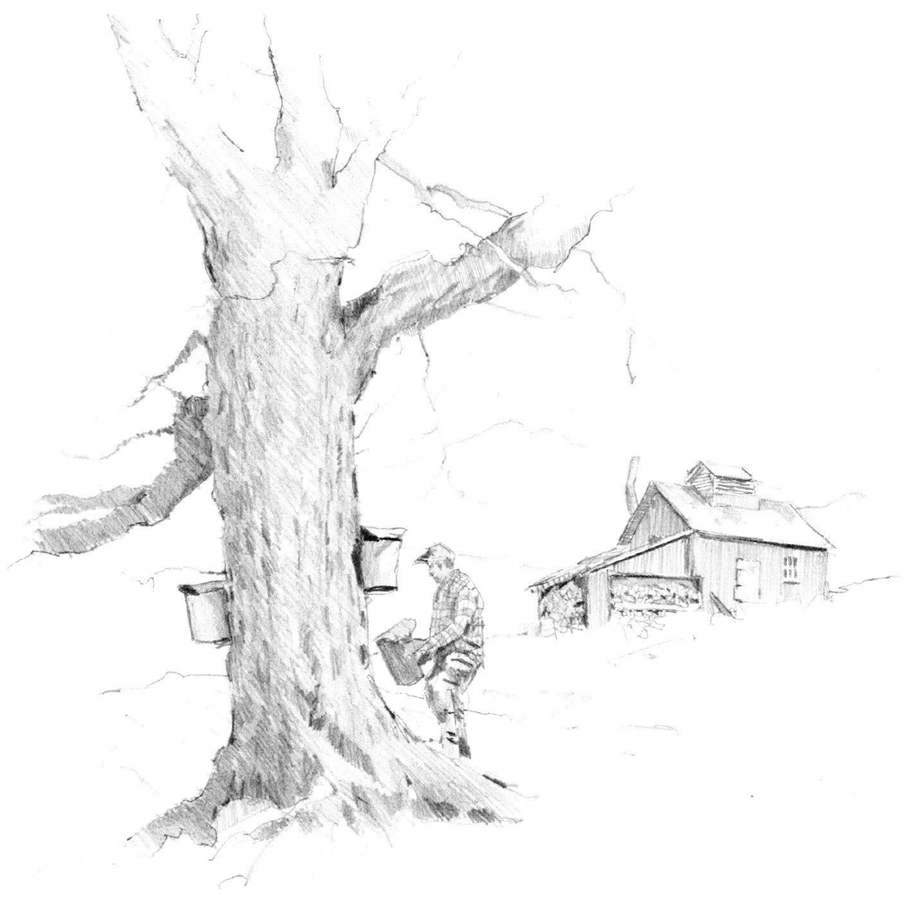

The shifting light on snow allows you to paint an abstract design. In the composition, the white allows your eye to move more easily to other parts of the painting, so it lends itself to a harmonious design.

Living on the coast we do not usually get as much snow as they do inland, especially up north. Our air temperature is usually several degrees warmer, so when western and northern New England are white, we are often just wet. Many nights I wait like a child on Christmas Eve for the flakes to fall, only to wake up to the sound of rain.

When it does snow, Rockport is as good as any place in New England to paint. Often I paint from morning until sunset in the streets and coves of Cape Ann. Much of what I see has not changed in one hundred years.

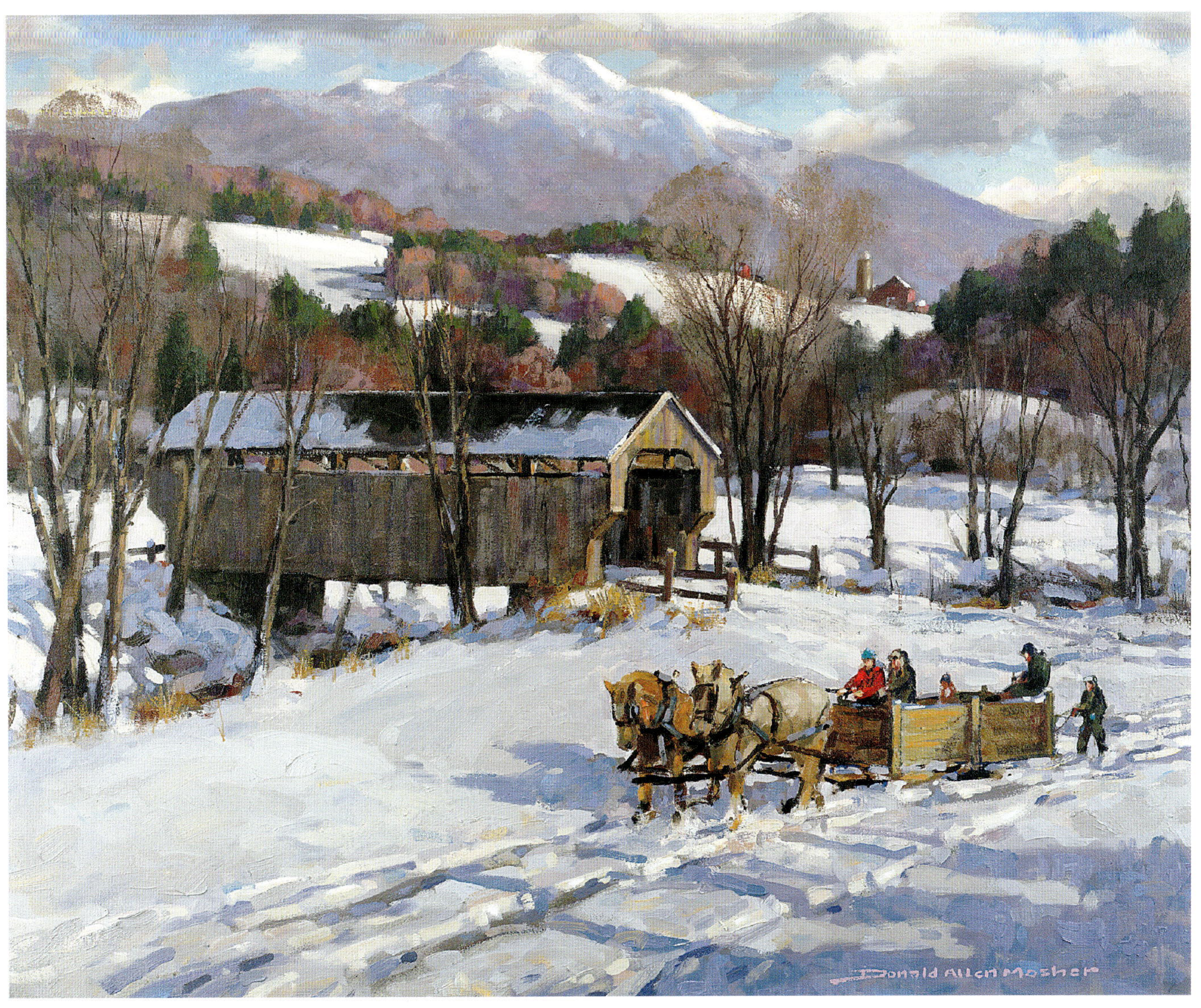

North Country Sleigh Ride (30 x 36)

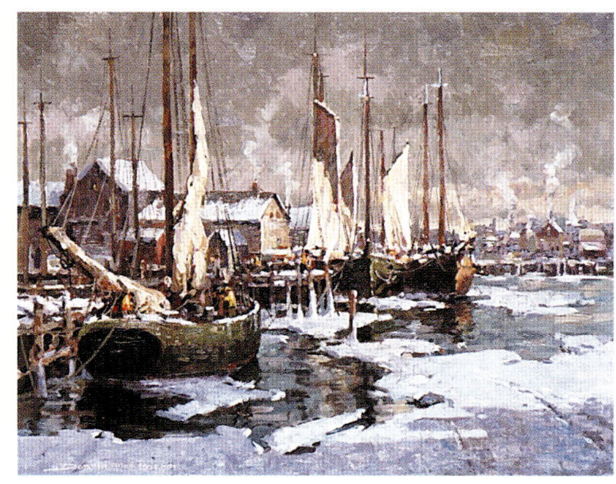

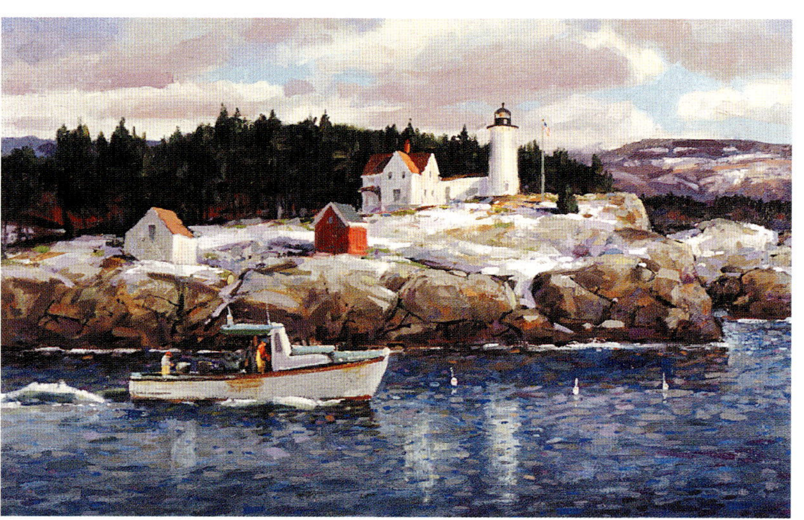

Top left: Study for "Drying Sails, Winter" (16 x 20)
Top right: Winter Cruise (20 x 30)

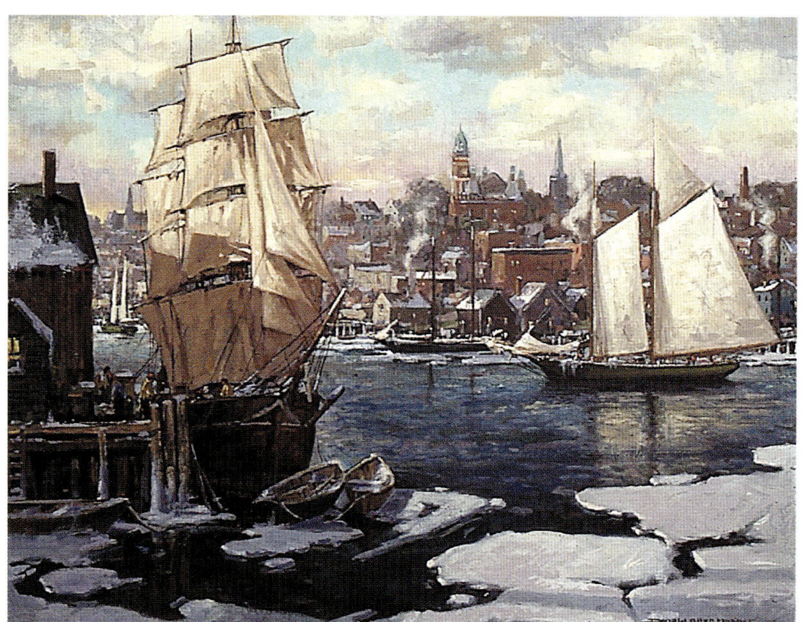

Bottom: Memories of Winter (30 x 38)

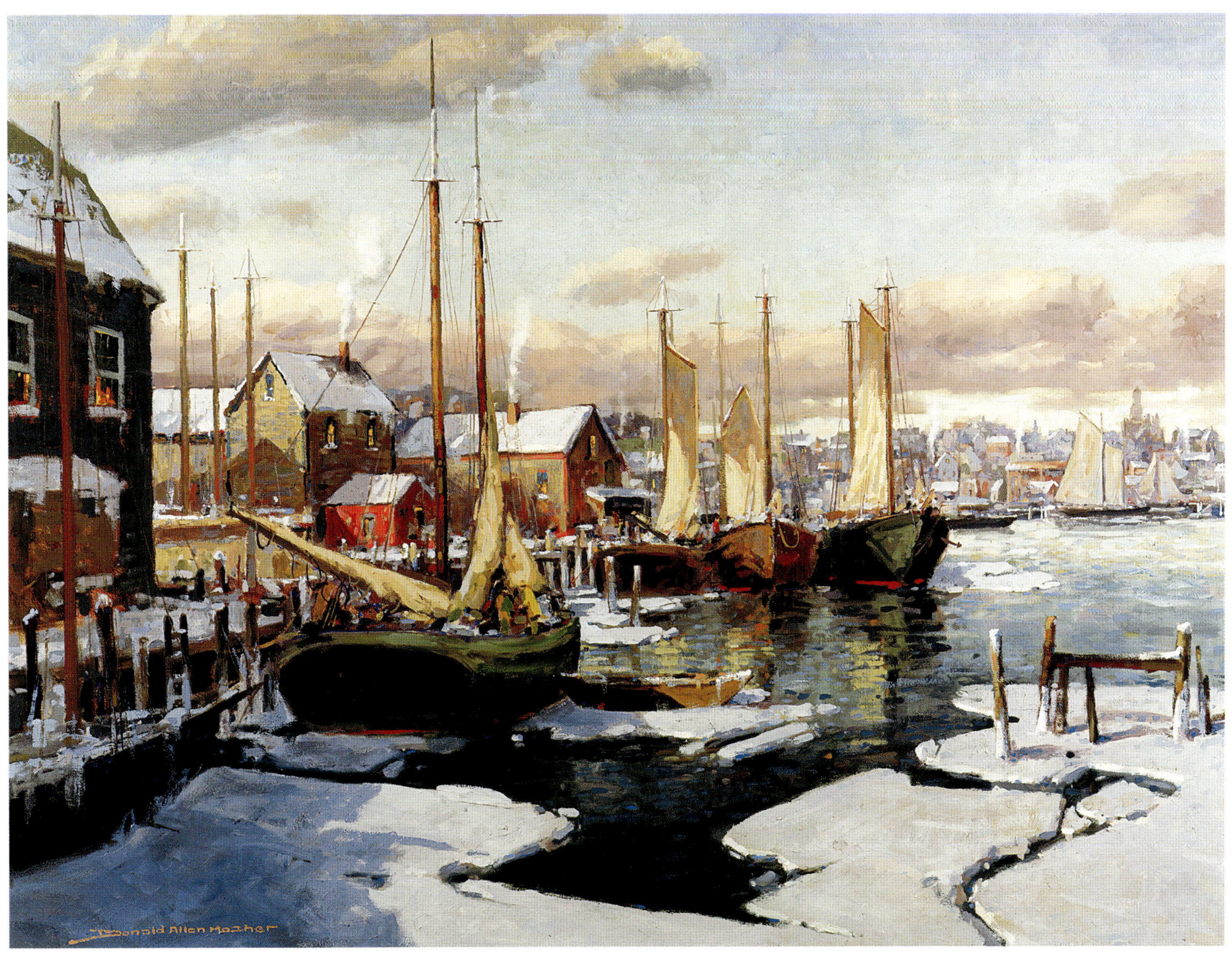

Drying Sails, Winter (30 x 38)

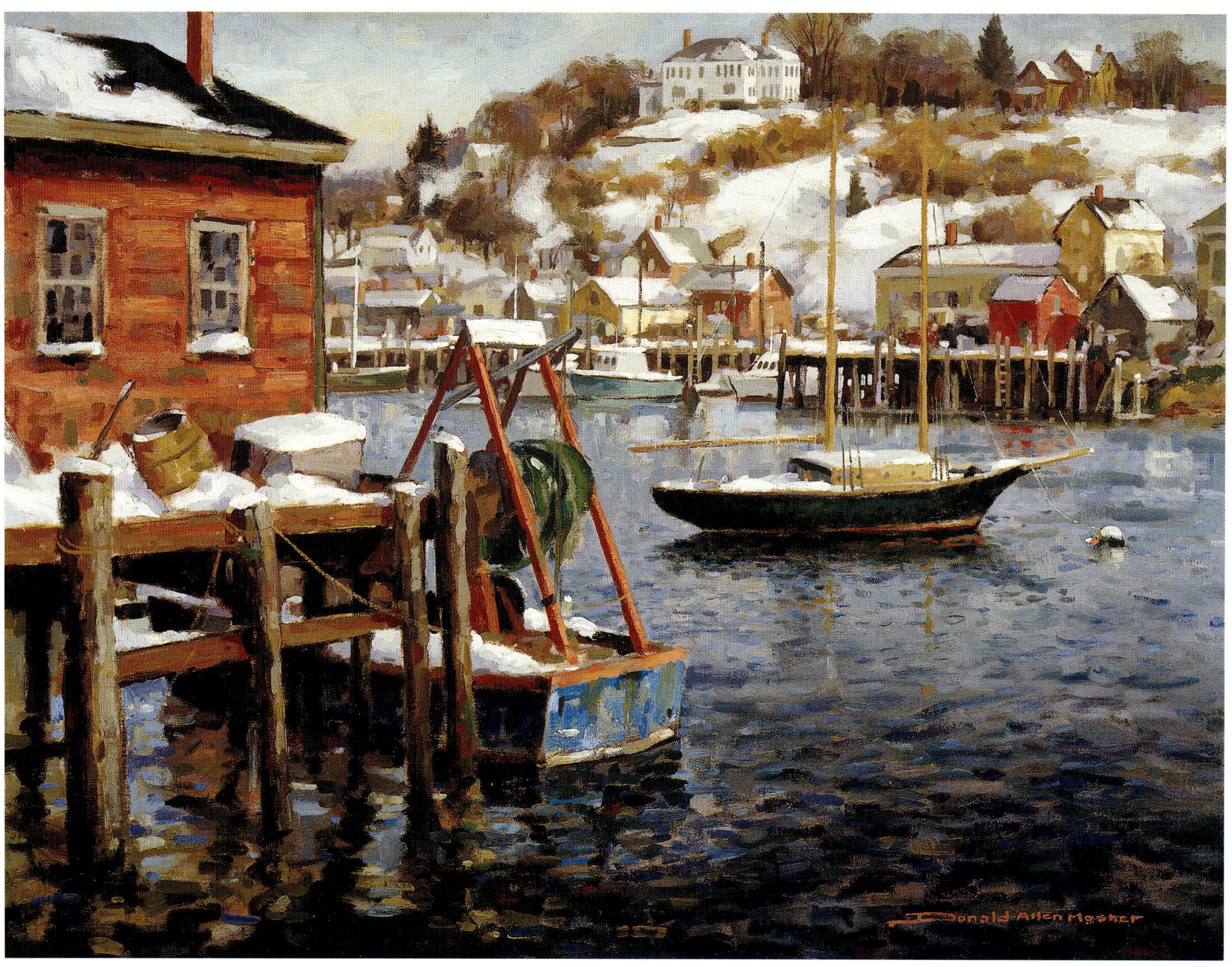

From Rocky Neck (25 x 30)

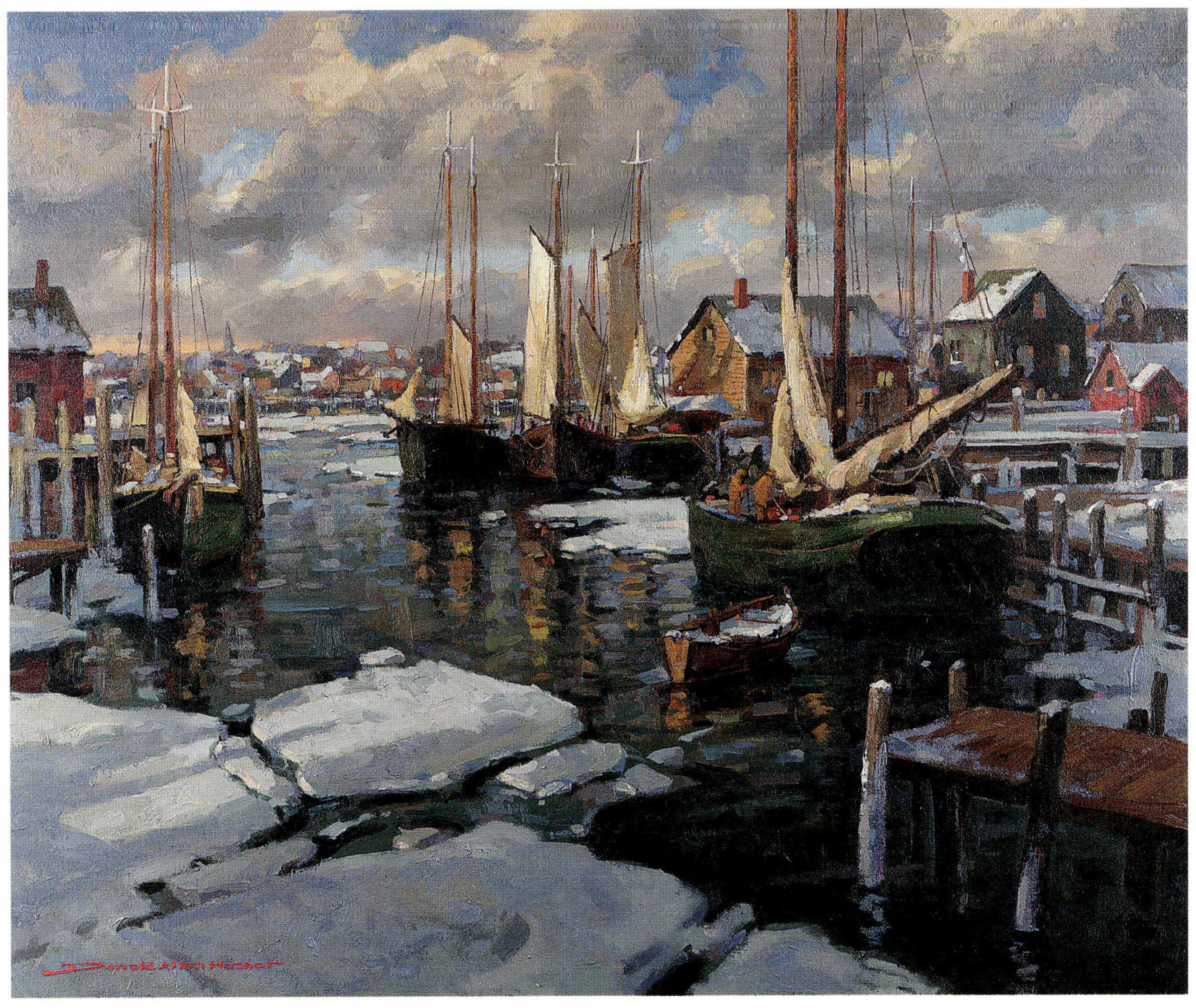

Frozen Harbor, Gloucester (30 x 36)

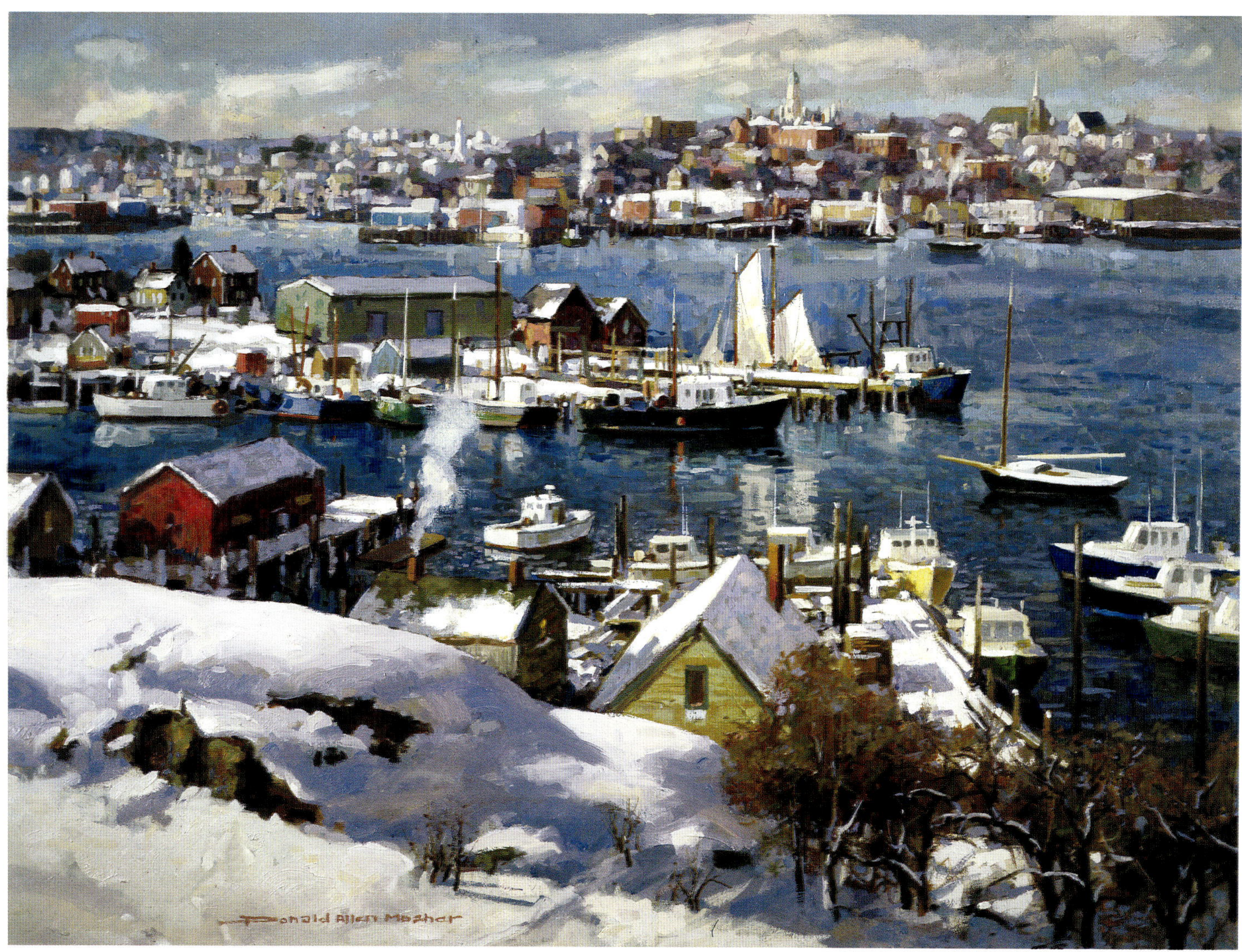

Winter Overlook (30 x 40)

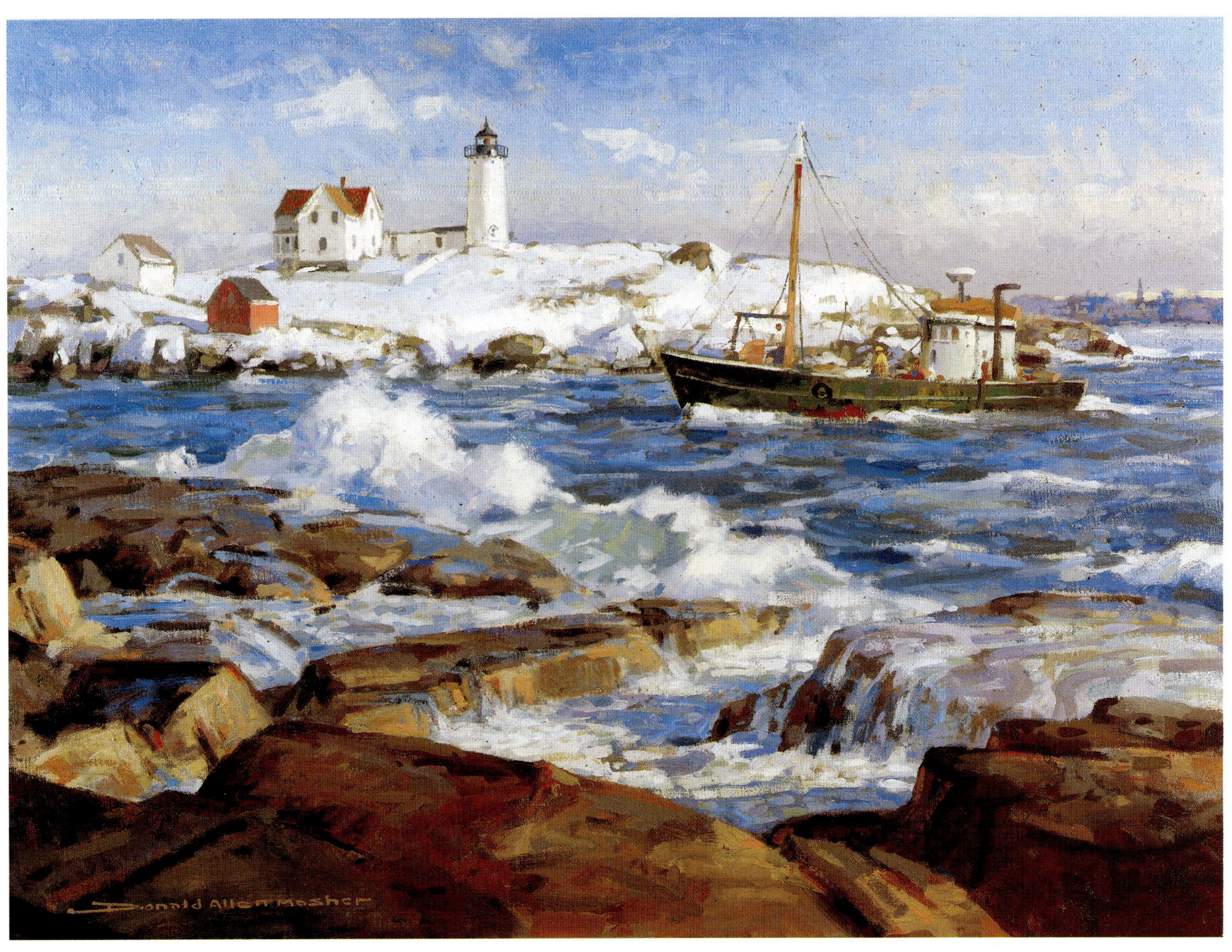

Nubble Light (24 x 30)

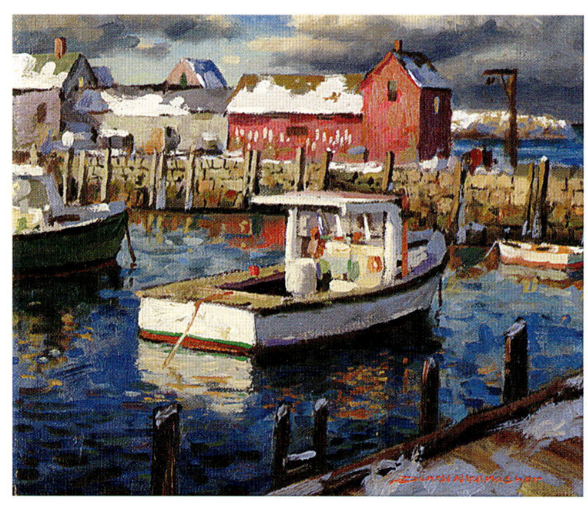

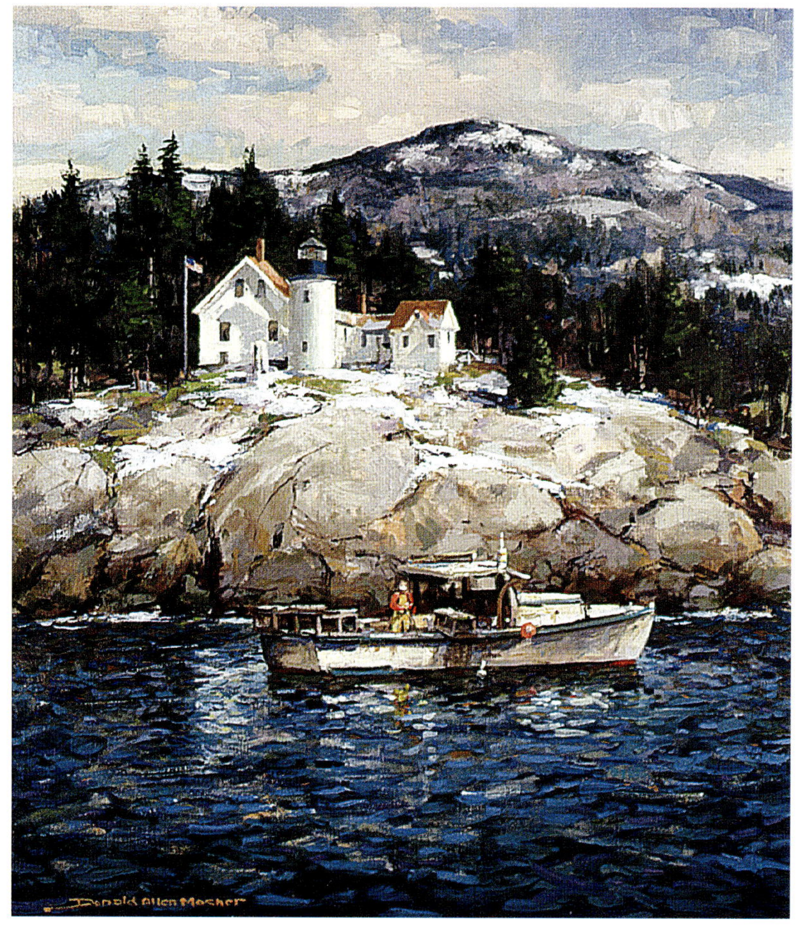

Left: Waiting for the Thaw (10 x 12)
Right: Hauling Traps, Maine (28 x 22)

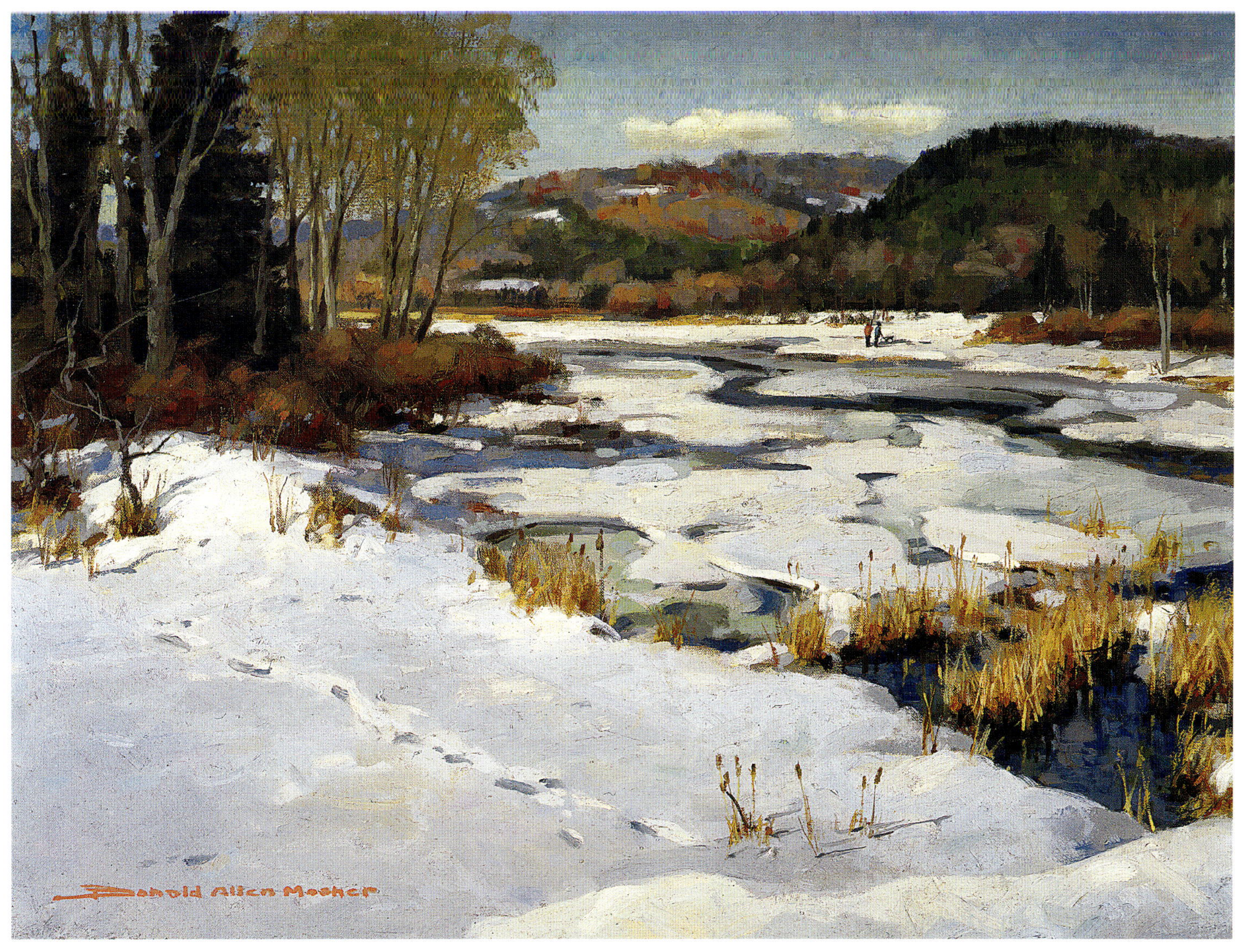

Sandy Neck, Maine (24 x 30)

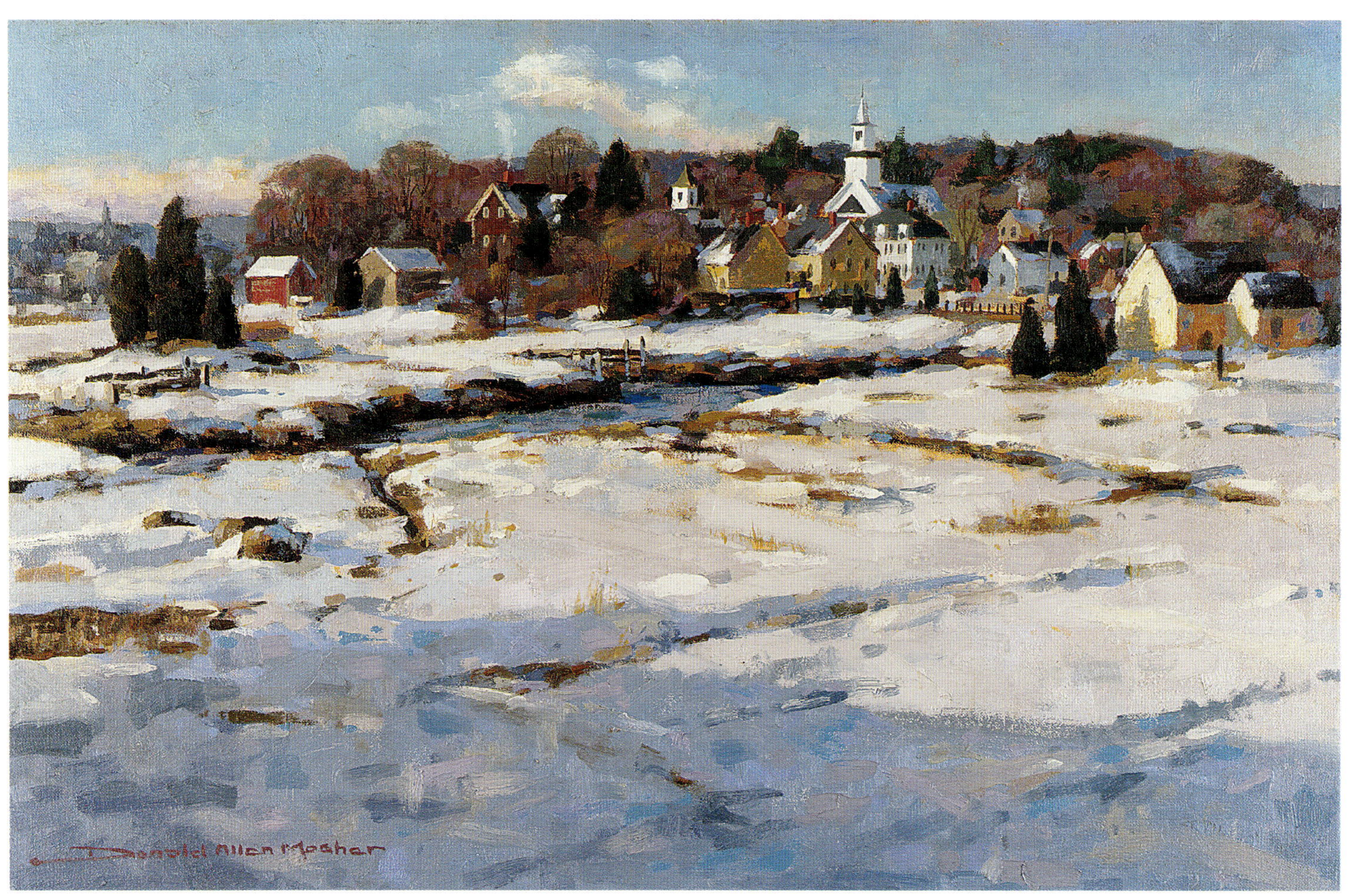

Frozen Marsh, Essex (20 x 30)

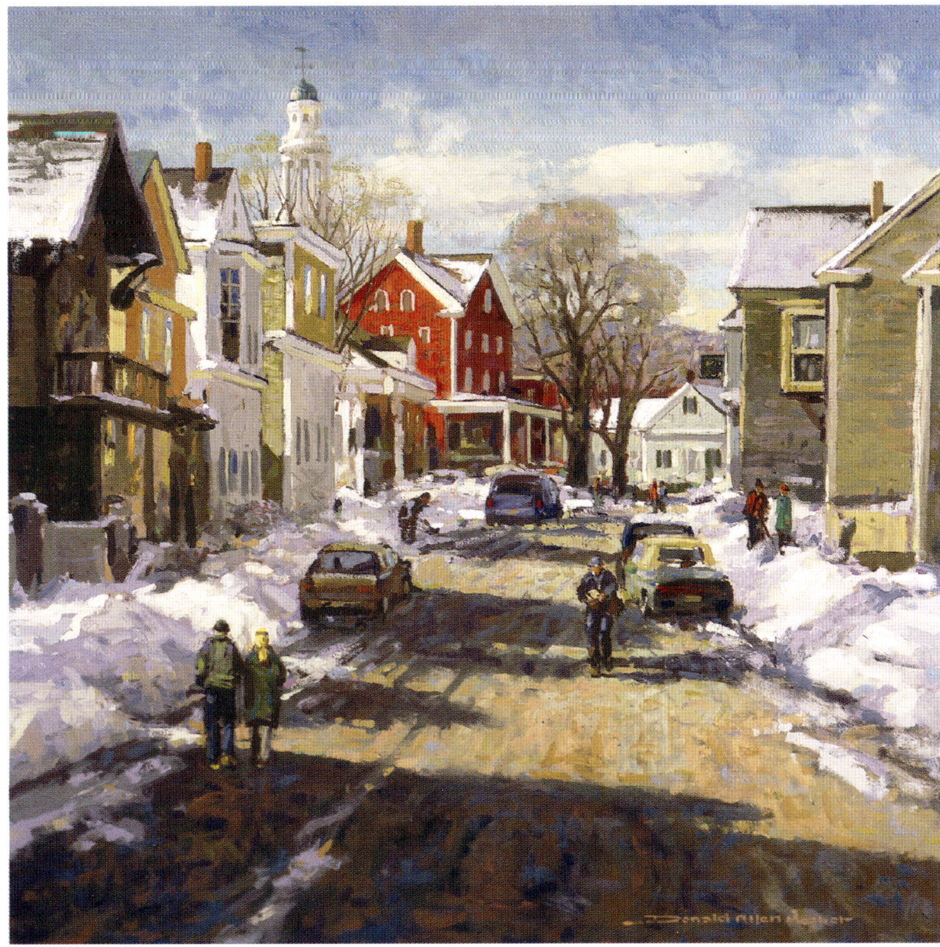

Originality cannot be sought after. It will come out when you express your conviction. Never be afraid of losing your individuality. If you have something personal to say, you will not be able to hide it.

—John Sloan

Shoveling Out, Dock Square, Rockport
(30 x 36)

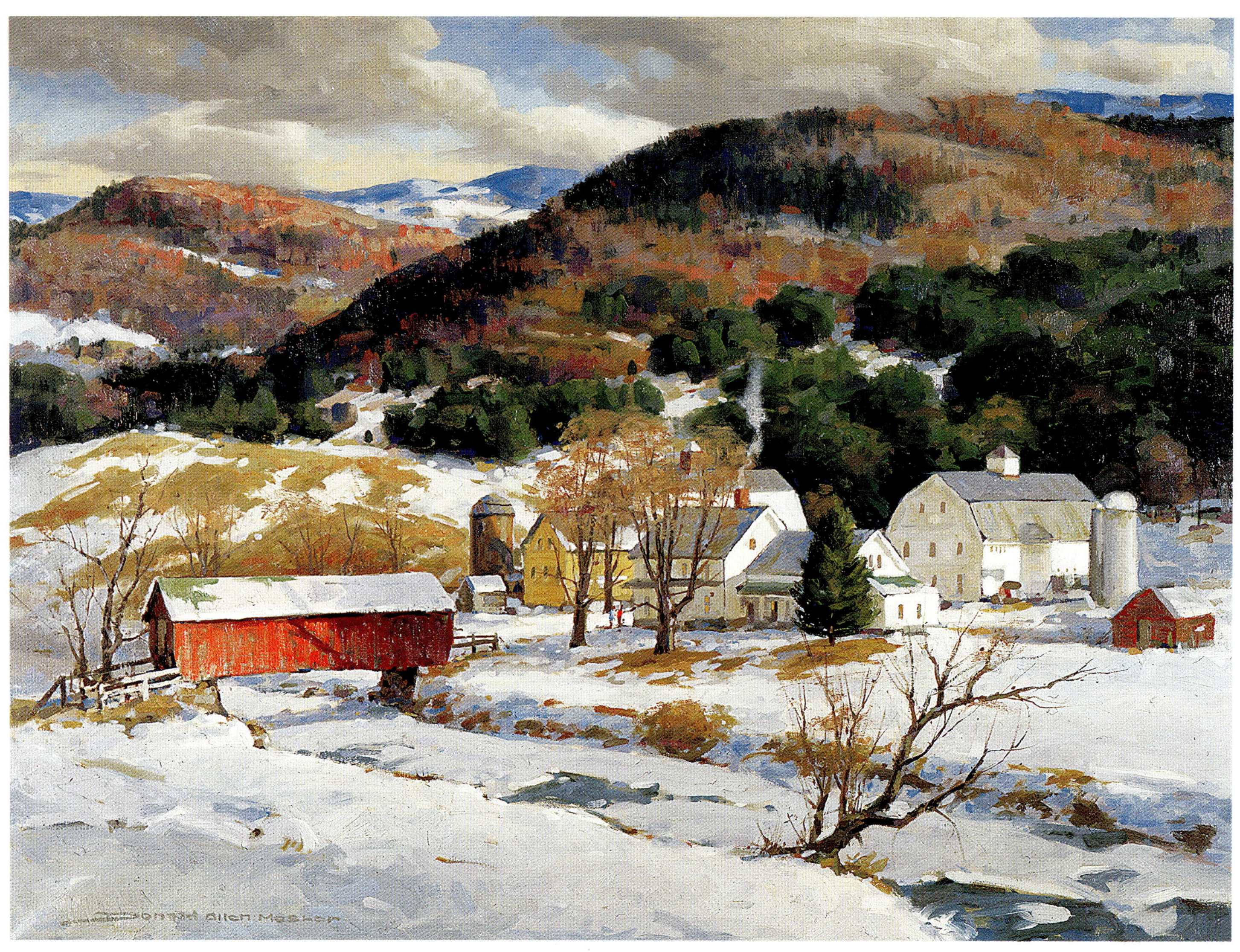

White Christmas (26 x 32)

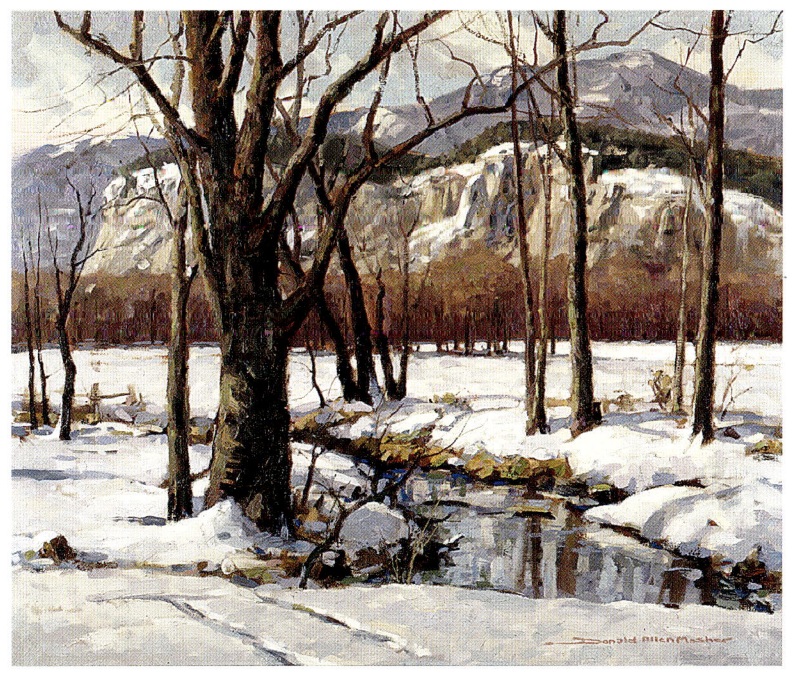

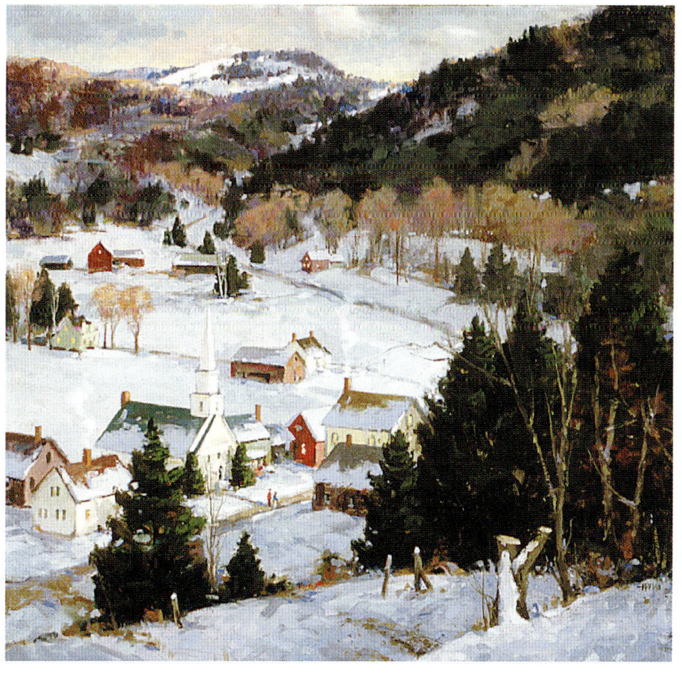

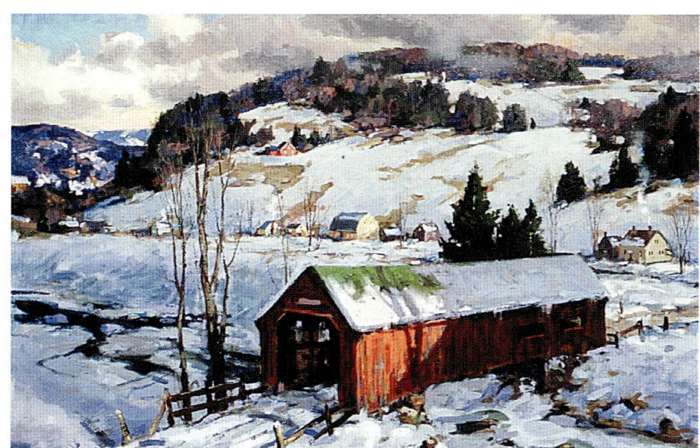

Top left: March Thaw, North Conway (25 x 30)
Top right: The Village Voice (16 x 16)
Bottom: Across the River (14 x 18)

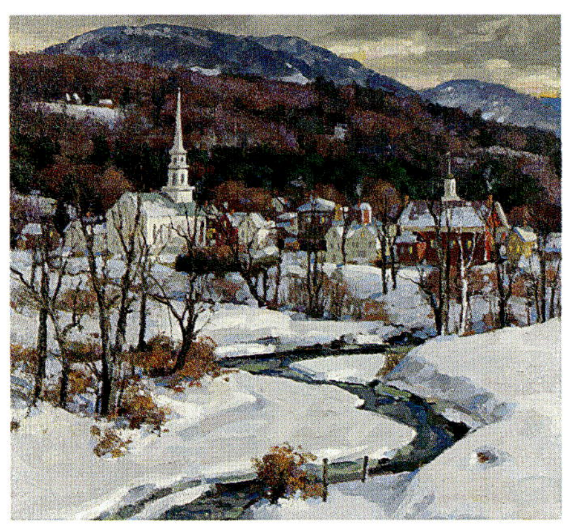

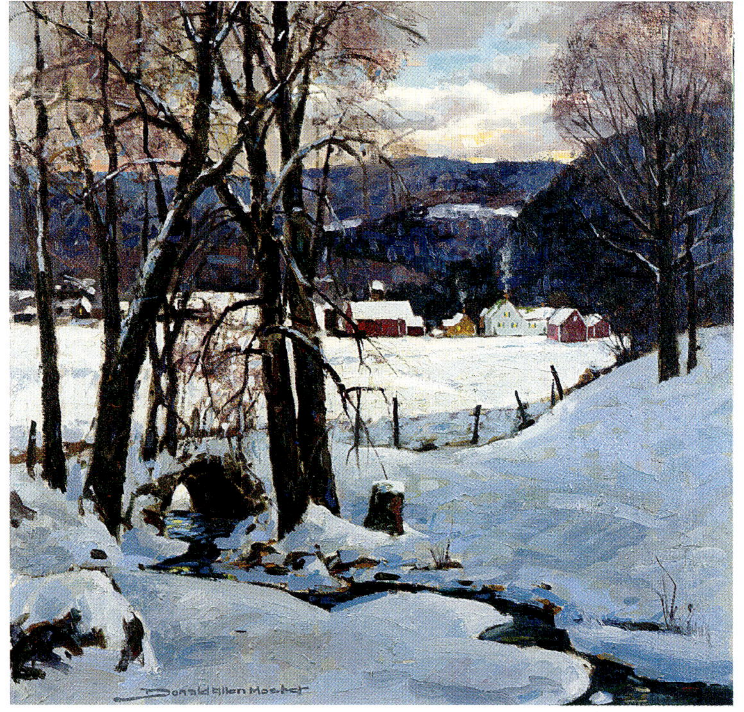

Top: Stowe, Vermont (20 x 20)
Bottom: Quiet Shadows (20 x 20)

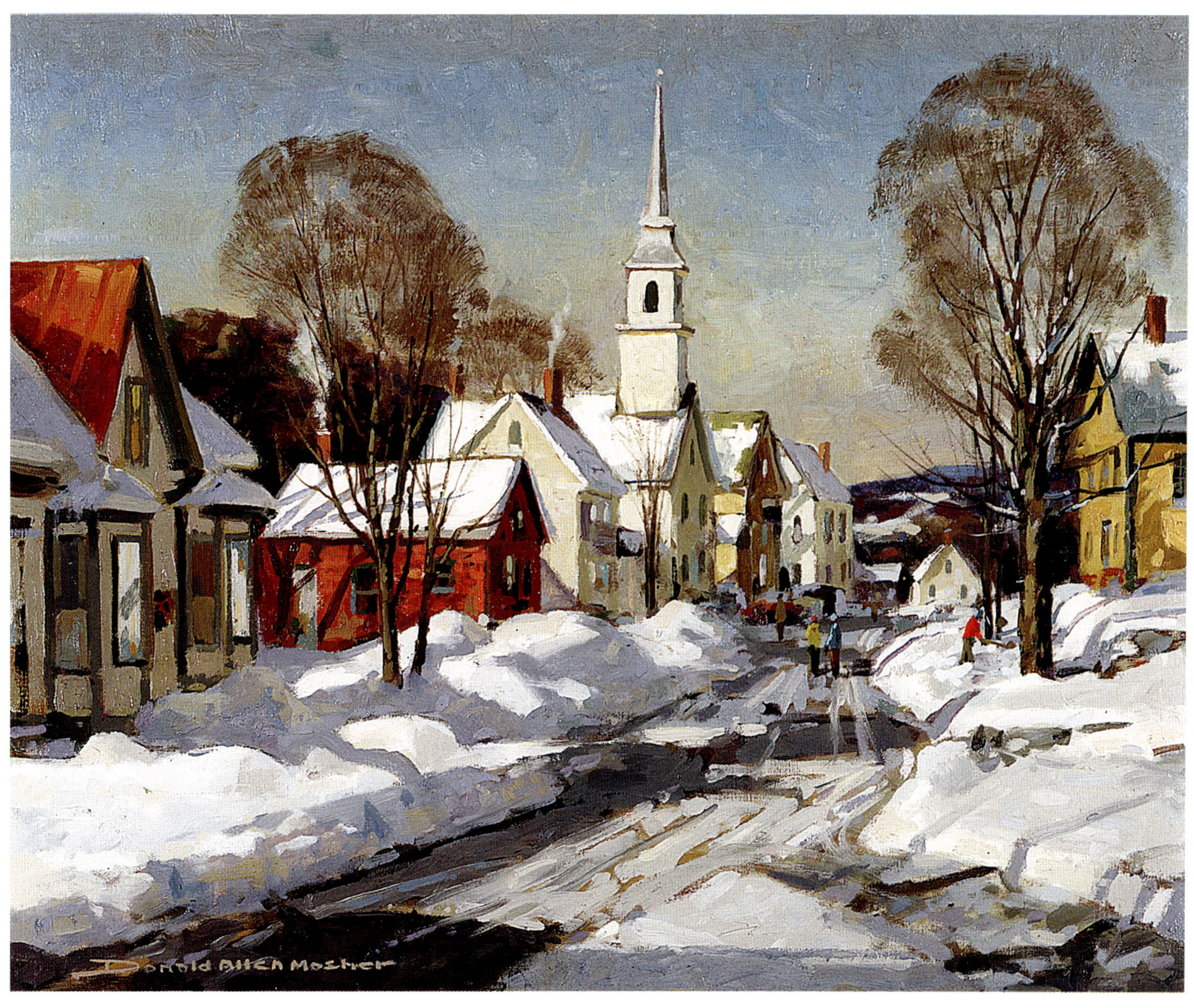

East Corinth, Vermont (20 x 24)

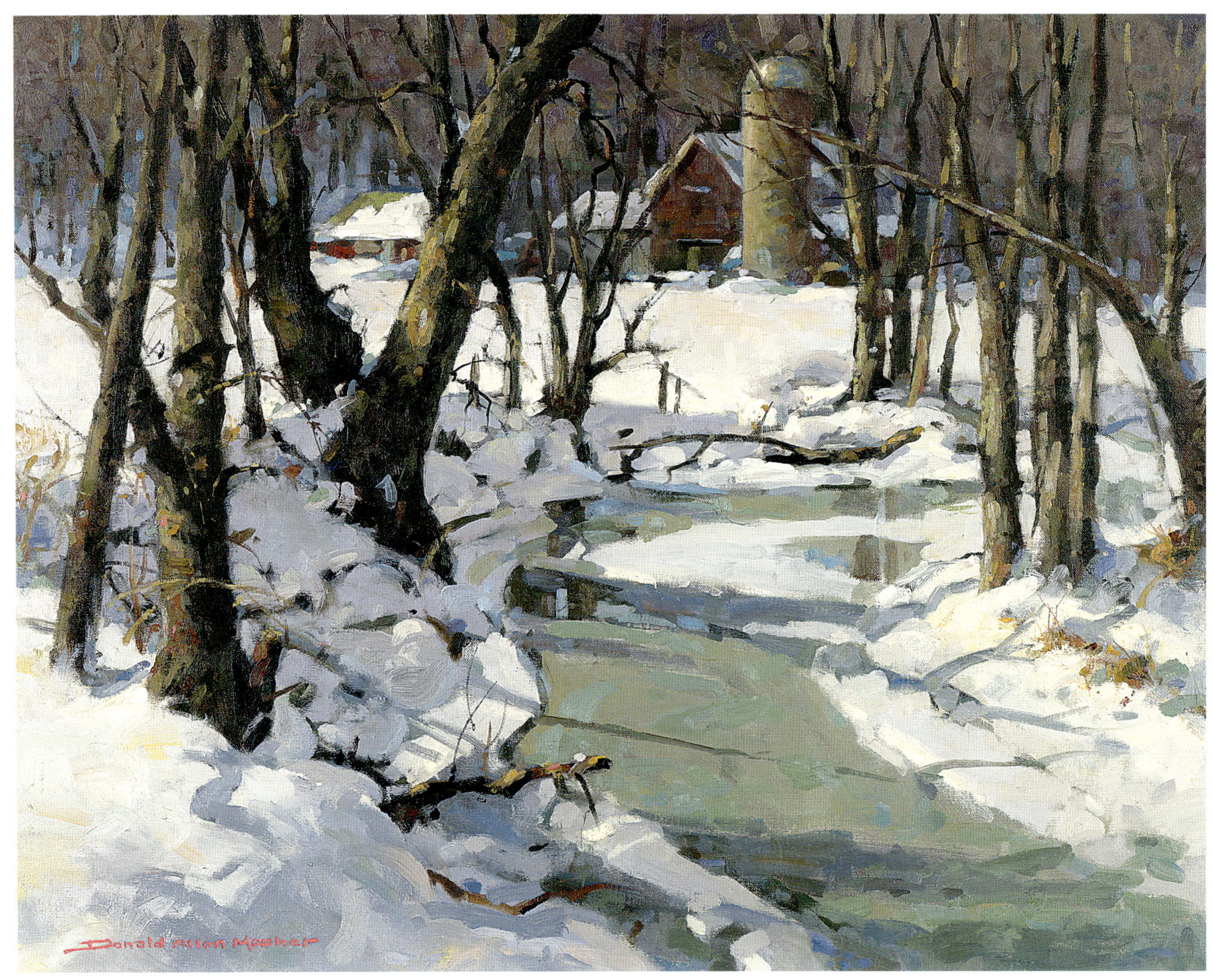

The Guardians (25 x 30)

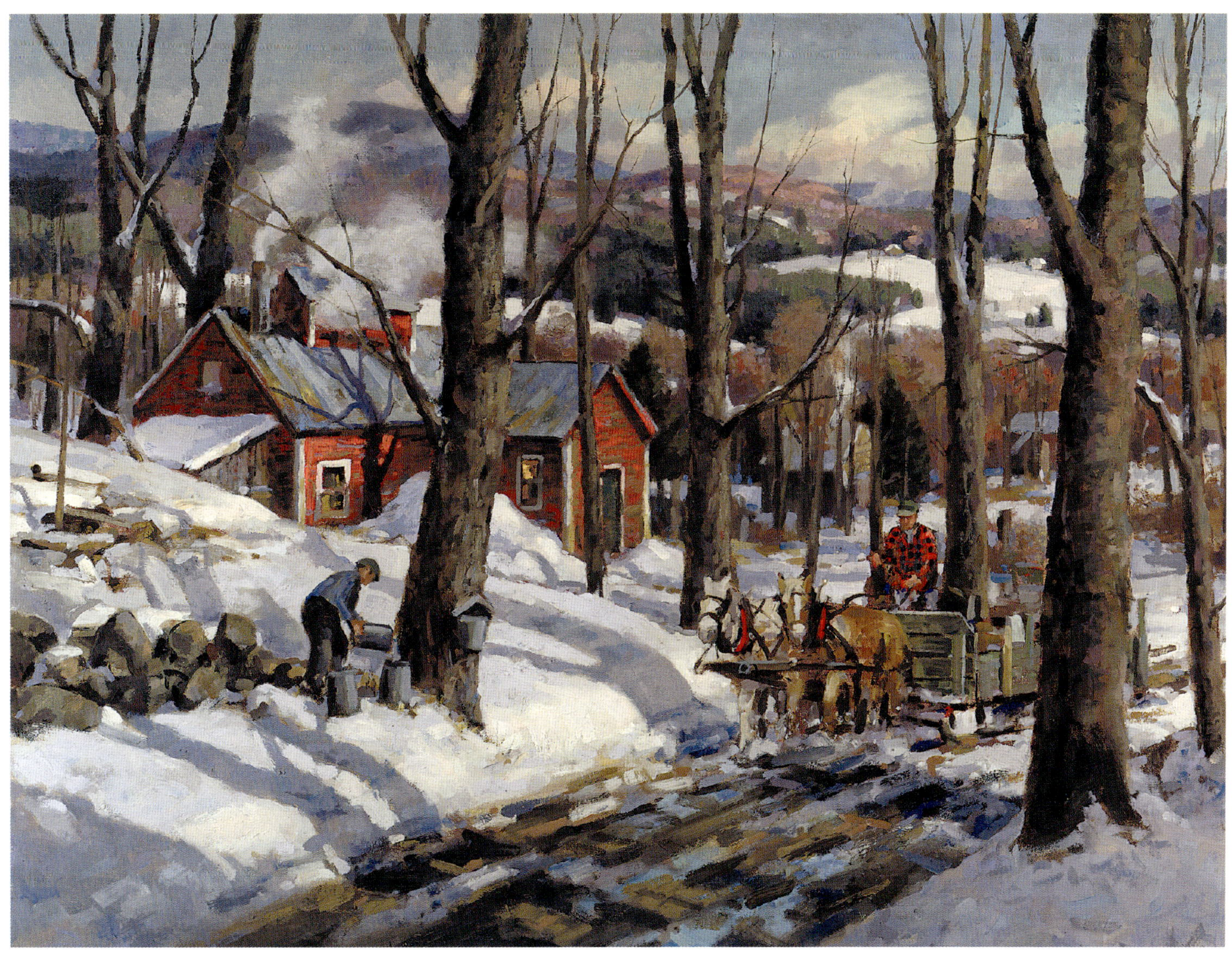

Gathering Sap (32 x 40)

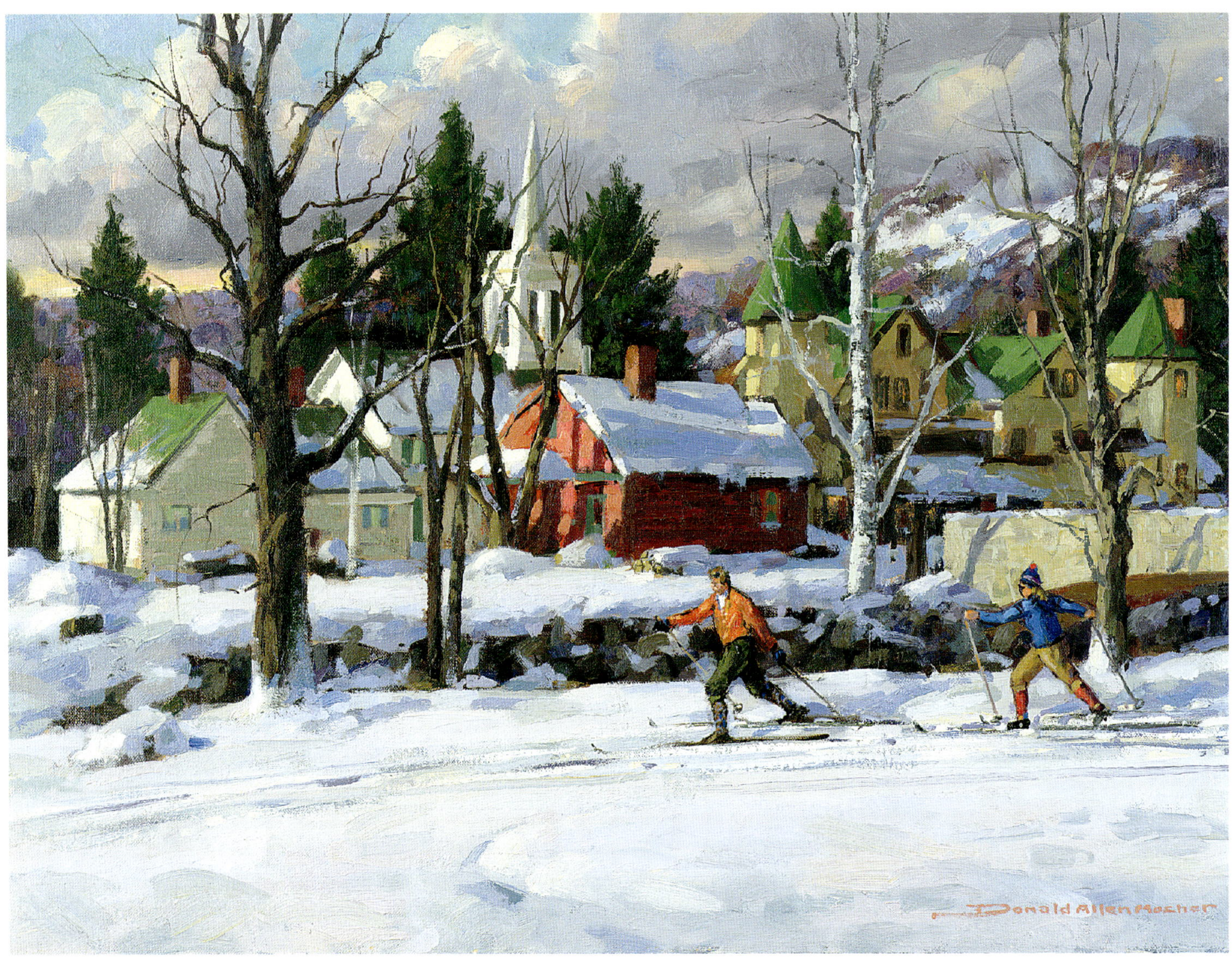

Jackson Ski Tour (20 x 30)

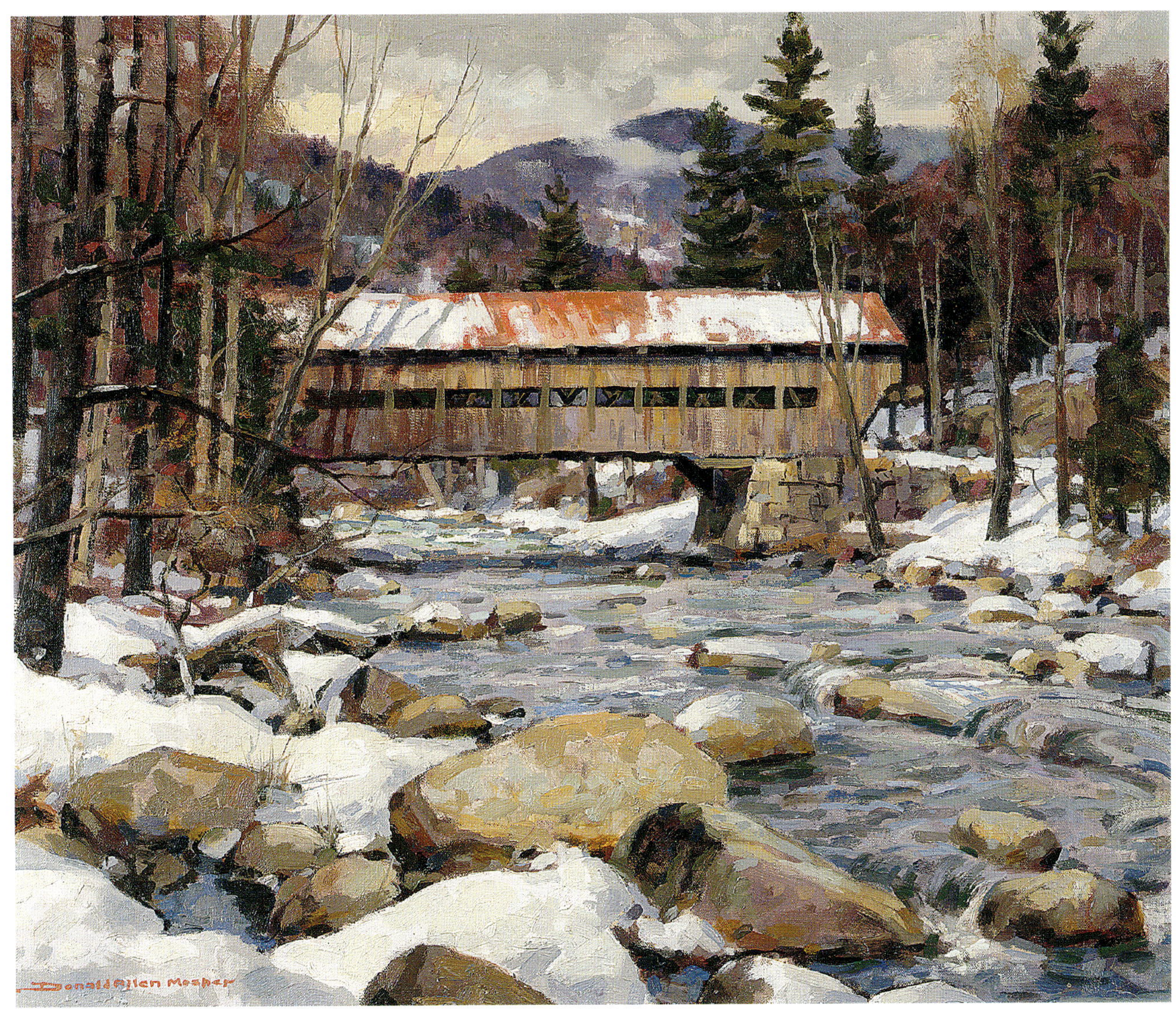

Winter on the Kancamagus (25 x 30)

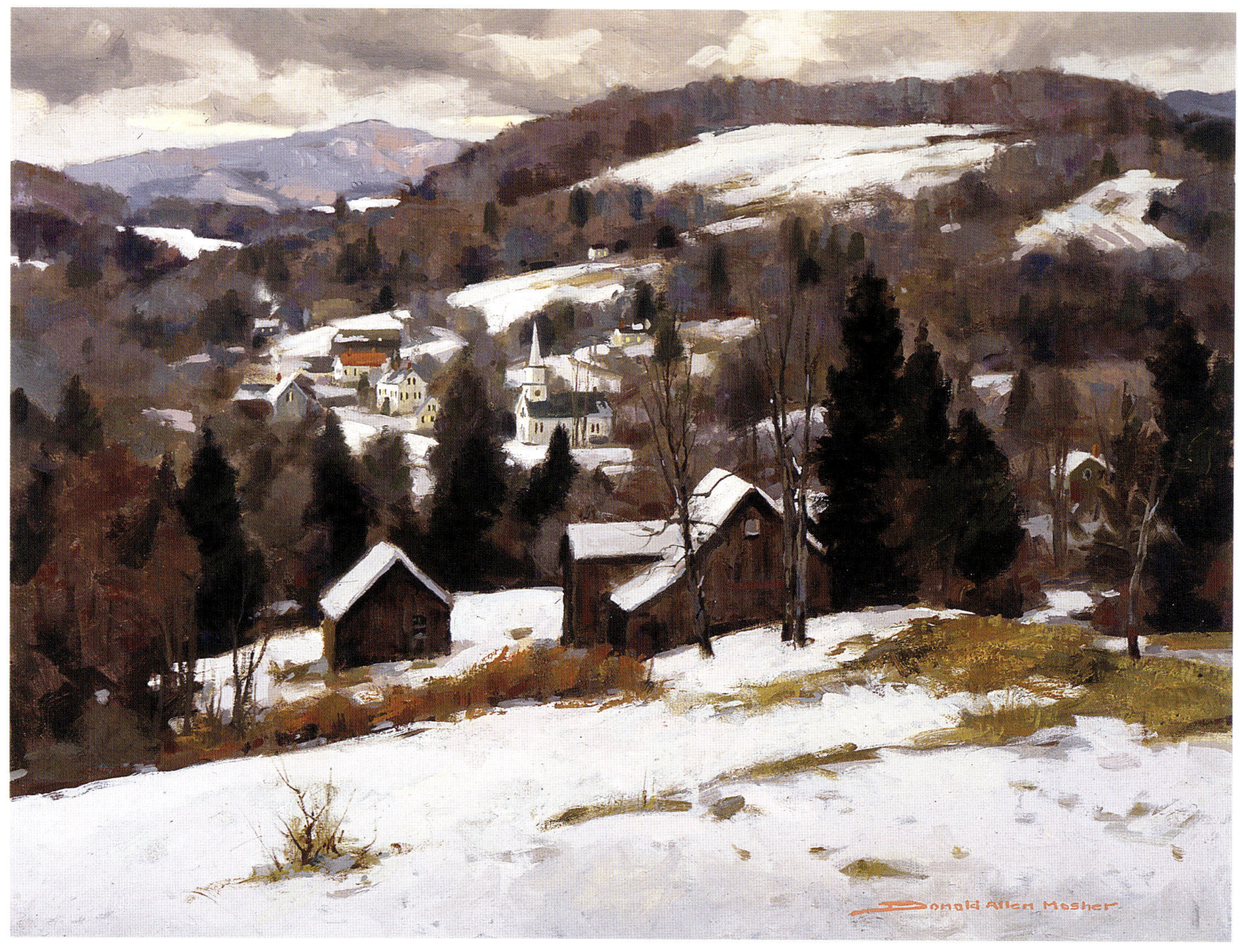

Gray Day, Vermont (25 x 30)

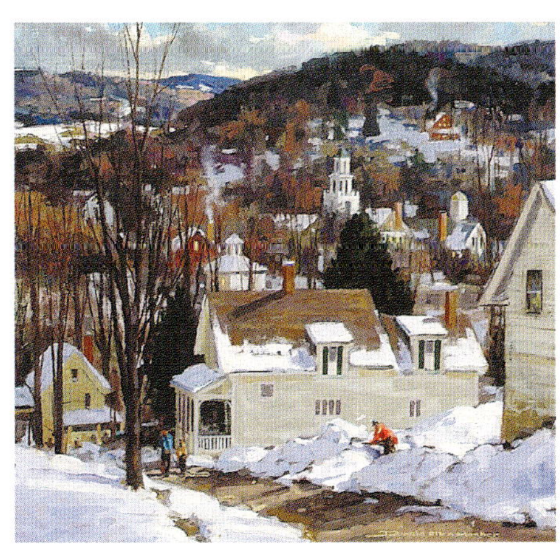

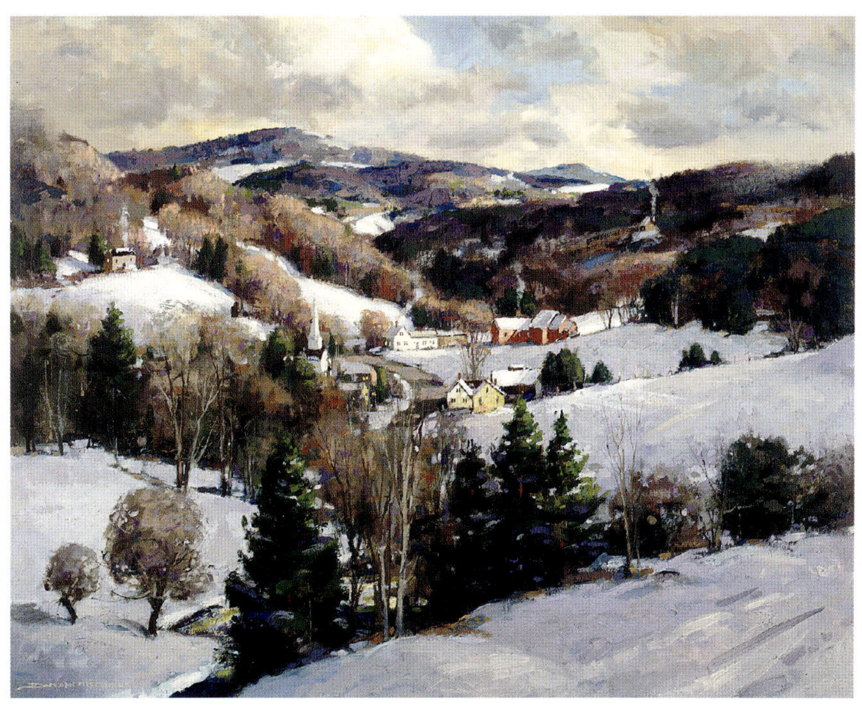

Top: Over Woodstock (20 x 20)
Bottom: Valley of a Thousand Paintings (20 x 24)

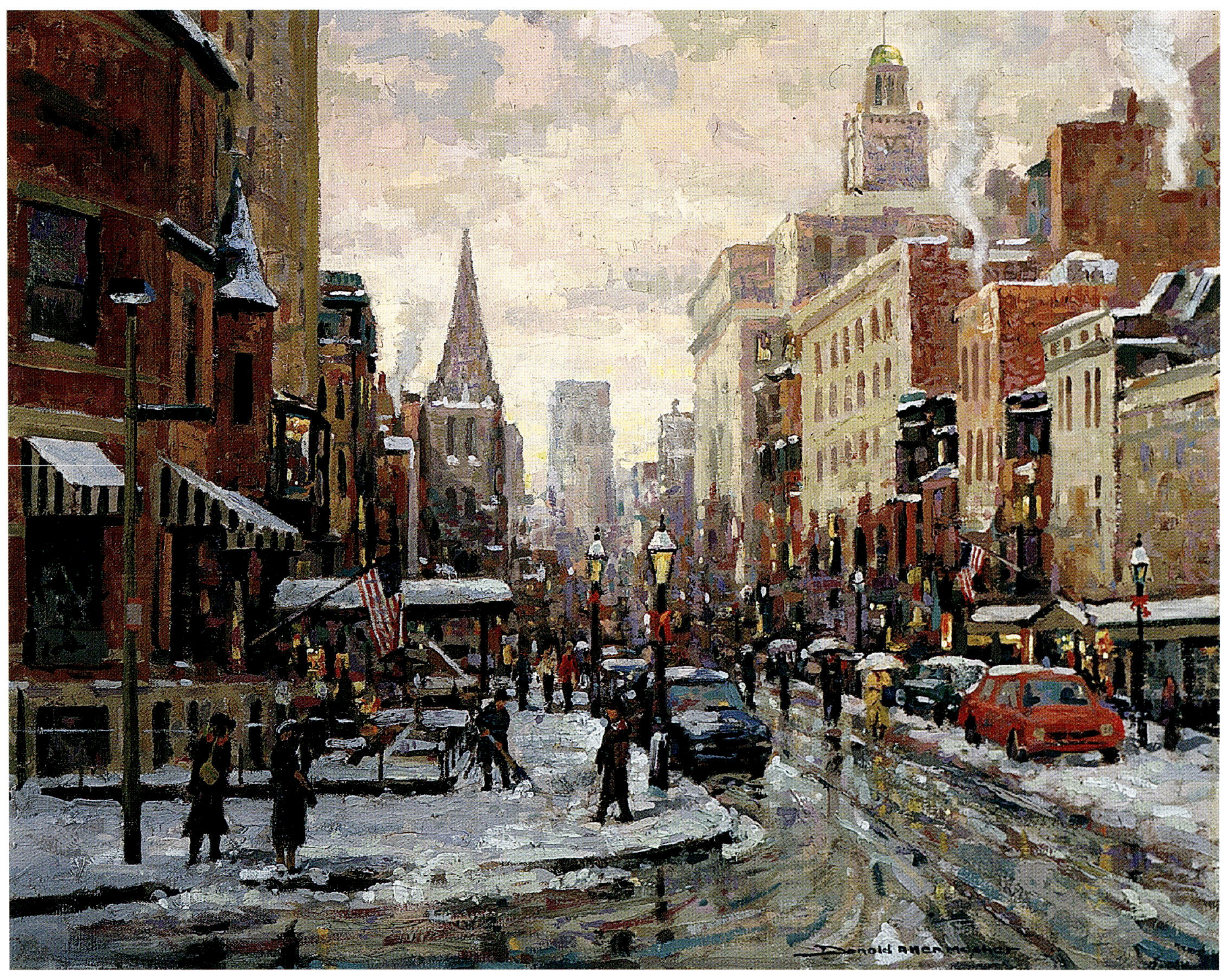

Newbury Street, Boston (24 x 30)

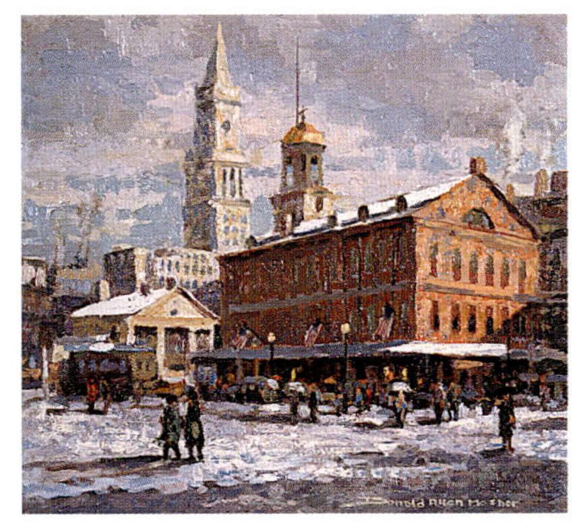

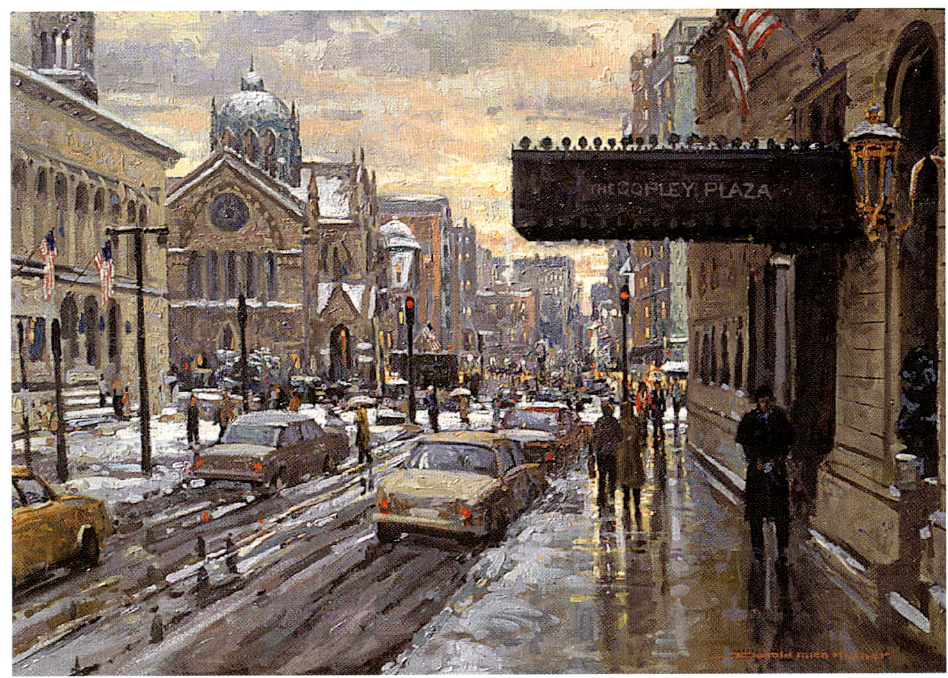

Top: Old Haymarket (16 x 16)
Bottom: Copley Square (26 x 36)

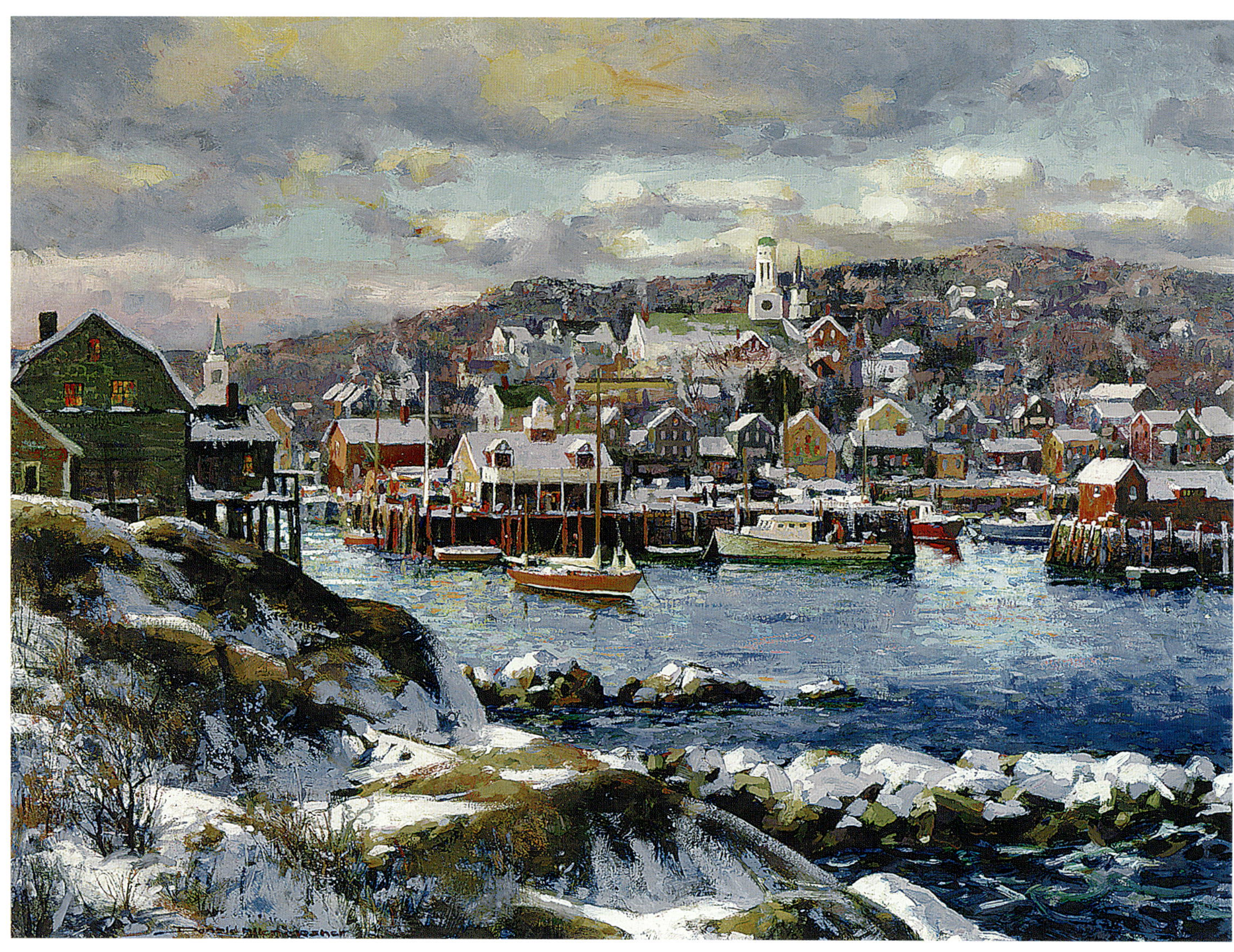

Winter Retreat, Rockport (30 x 36)

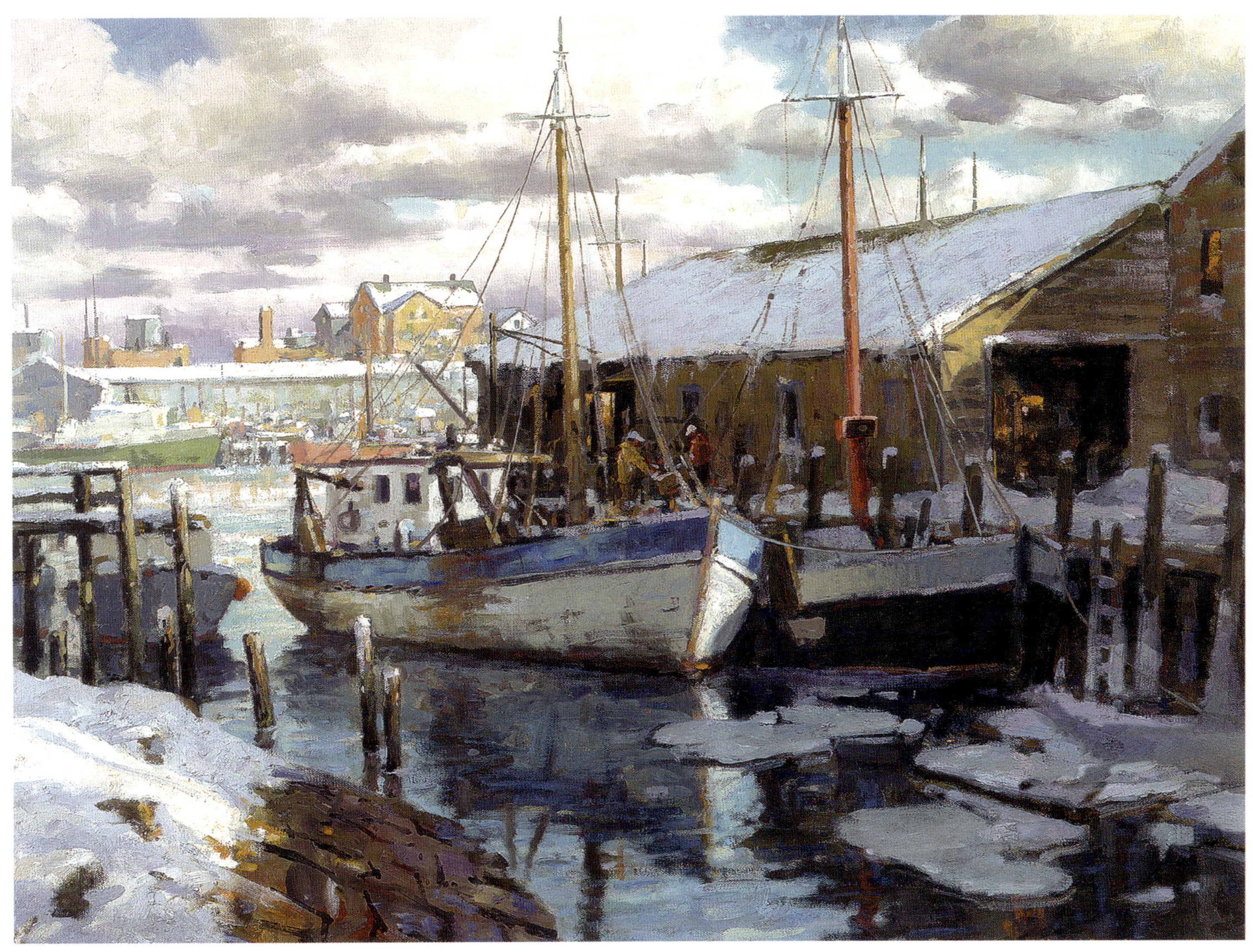

Fisherman's Wharf (24 x 30)

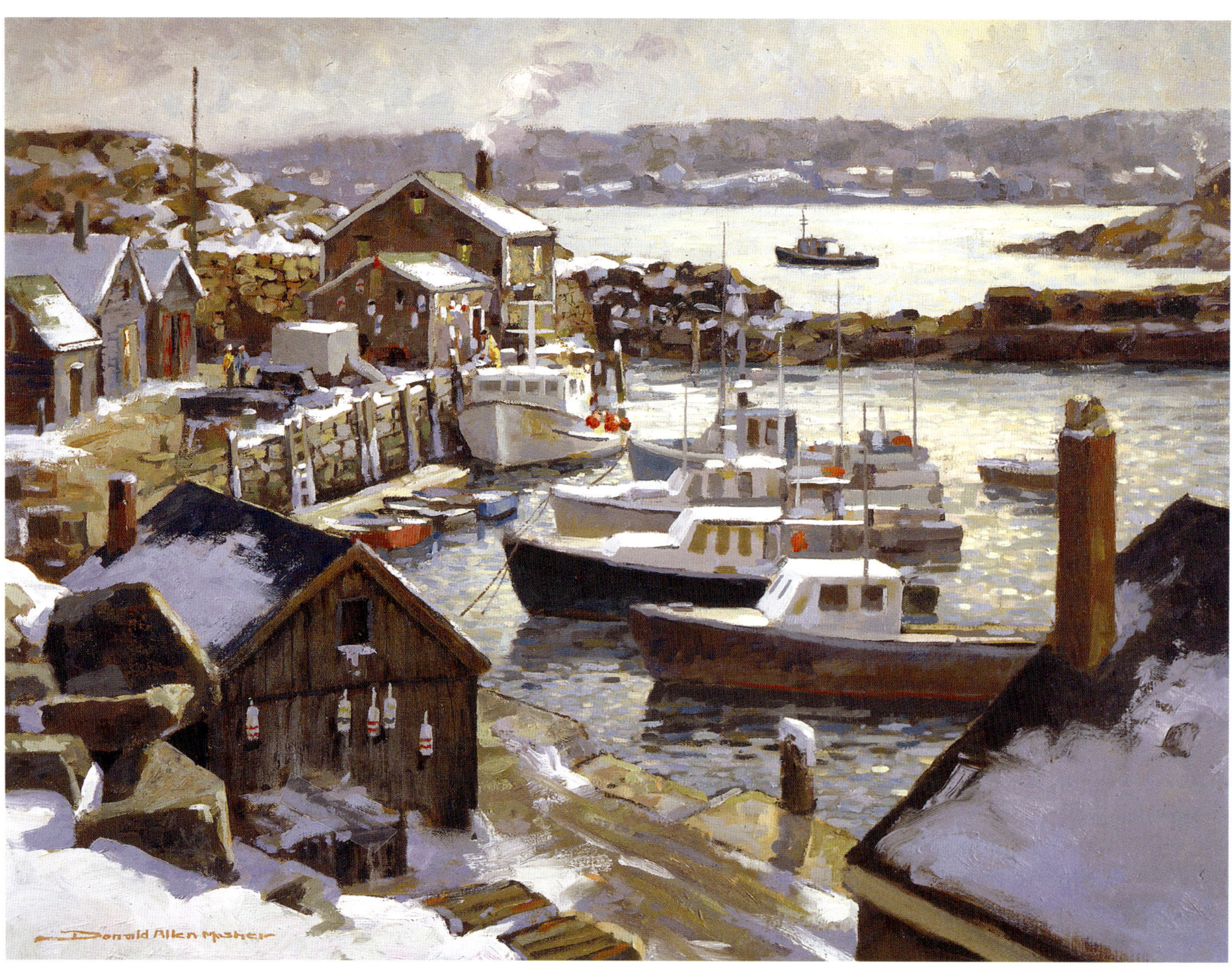

Winter, Pigeon Cove, Rockport (25 x 30)

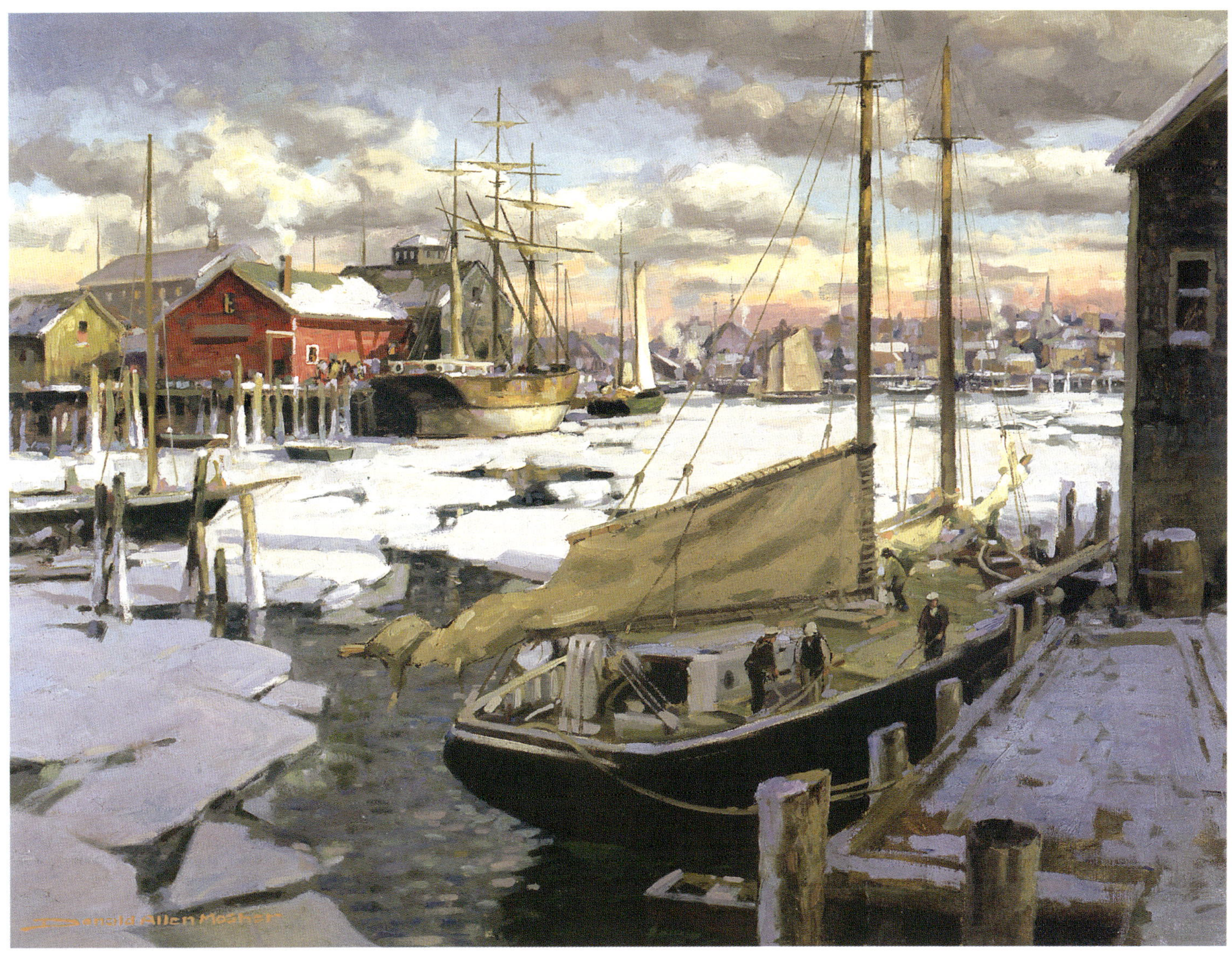

The End of an Era (34 x 40)

THE MOSHER GALLERY

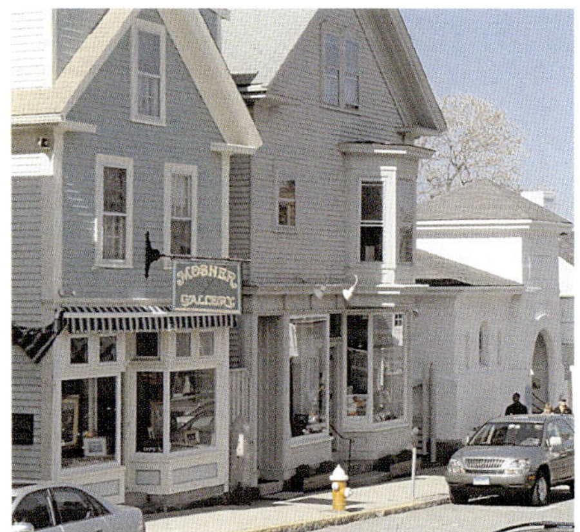

The Mosher Gallery, 13 Main Street, Rockport, Massachusetts

Over thirty years ago, Don Mosher and his wife, Christine, made the decision to devote their lives to art. This not only meant years spent in the arduous study of technique, but also required the willingness to become involved in one of the chanciest lifestyles imaginable.

To help pay for his education, Don spent his nights driving a taxi in Boston. After graduating from art school, he worked as an art director. Eventually, he decided that the security of a regular job prevented him from doing what really mattered—his own work, in his own time, at his own pace. Don and Christine took one of the biggest gambles of their lives: he quit his job and together they sold their home and bought a gallery in downtown Rockport. In the beginning, they lived in an apartment over the shop.

The rich art history of Cape Ann began to have a greater effect on Don's work. He had always admired the Cape Ann School, but now he began an intense study of their work, seeking it out in books, private collections, and exhibitions. He soon developed his own approach to painting: a combination of the dedicated outdoor work favored by his Cape Ann predecessors, combined with intense and thoughtful work in the studio where he can spend the time necessary to clarify his plein-air inspiration.

All of Don's work is a testimony to his years of study, his dedication, and his complete devotion to the art of painting.

—Charles Movalli,
Gloucester, Massachusetts